About the Author

After boarding school in Scotland and an accounting apprenticeship in England where he qualified with the ICAEW, Grant Tait was an auditor in London and Paris. By this time he had saved enough money to pay for an MBA at INSEAD in France.

His career continued in the European HQ of a US company in Paris, then three years in Switzerland as Finance Director. Thereafter, he worked in Europe with multinational companies for 35 years.

This involved intensive travel which was fun. Travel included projects abroad: distribution agreements in Tokyo and Amsterdam, new offices in Barcelona, fraud in Geneva, and meetings all over the world. He managed teams in USA, and around Europe.

In his 30s, he wrote articles making fun of management decisions in multinationals. They were published in various professional magazines such as *Management Today*, *Personnel Journal* and *Management Accounting*. However, to protect his job, he had to write anonymously because his company could be identified.

He worked for several bosses who never made decisions. This resulted in his first book after he retired: *How to become a no-decision manager* which won a silver medal from the Non-Fiction Authors Association in USA.

Also by Grant Tait

Non-fiction

How to Become a No-Decision Manager

FUN WITH ACCOUNTANTS
Searching for the Silly in the Serious

Grant Tait

SilverWood

Published in 2024 by SilverWood Books

SilverWood Books Ltd
14 Small Street, Bristol, BS1 1DE, United Kingdom
www.silverwoodbooks.co.uk

Copyright © Grant Tait 2024

The right of Grant Tait to be identified as the author of this
work has been asserted in accordance with the Copyright,
Designs and Patents Act 1988 Sections 77 and 78.

All rights reserved. No part of this publication may be reproduced,
stored in a retrieval system, or transmitted in any form or by any means,
electronic, mechanical, photocopying, recording or otherwise,
without prior permission of the copyright holder.

ISBN 978-1-80042-285-8 (paperback)
Also available as an ebook

British Library Cataloguing in Publication Data
A CIP catalogue record for this book is available from the British Library

Page design and typesetting by SilverWood Books

IFRS® Foundation Copyright and Disclaimer Notice
This publication contains copyright material of the IFRS® Foundation in respect of which all rights are reserved. Reproduced by SilverWood Books Ltd with the permission of the IFRS Foundation. No permission granted to third parties to reproduce or distribute. For full access to IFRS Standards and the work of the IFRS Foundation please visit http://ifrs.org. The International Accounting Standards Board, the IFRS Foundation, the authors and the publishers do not accept responsibility for any loss caused by acting or refraining from acting in reliance on the material in this publication, whether such loss is caused by negligence or otherwise.

To Liz and Nicole, for their patience

Not funny as in hilarious, although it certainly had its amusing moments. But more funny as in unusual.

Agent in Berlin, Alex Gerlis

Contents

Fun with Acronyms	13
Fun with a Glossary	17
Introduction	21
Seven accounting sisters	22
More choice, more confusion	25
Conspirators	27
Disagreement on accounting standards	28
Sources of fun	29
Why the chapter headings?	32
Chapter 1 Entertaining Fun	35
JARGON	35
The bearer plant	35
Where is concern going?	36
Not only fair but also true	39
Accounting headroom	41
Why make deferred taxes so complicated?	43
STANDARDS	44
Refined material	44
Tied up in knots	48
The noble concept of the spectrum of inherent risk	50
The confusion around GAAP	52
ANNUAL REPORTS	53
Looking forward in a statement	53
Predict the unpredictable	56
An audit matters critically	58
Exaggeration, boasting and complication	59
FORMAL REPORTS	61
A number of approaches	61
Sinking feeling	64
Licence agreement of the FASB	65

Chapter 2	**Silly Fun**	**70**
JARGON		70
	Accountants are concerned about going	70
	Lying under	72
	Unwinding the uplift	73
	Ride over management	75
	Clean or dirty	76
STANDARDS		77
	Material definitions differ	77
	Work together to make a frame	80
	If, and only if	82
	Accounting uncertainty	83
	The imaginary Chief Operating Decision Maker	86
	They cannot agree on an accounting principle?	87
ANNUAL REPORTS		90
	Respect of material	90
	An invaluable value to worry about	92
	Accountants can't make up their minds	94
	The rubber-stamp UKEB	98
	Material marks on the bench	100
FORMAL REPORTS		104
	Rollover the iron curtain	104
	Royal Charter	105
Chapter 3	**Amusing Fun**	**107**
JARGON		107
	A BIT of an E – an EBIT	107
	Accounting inputs	109
	Trigger happy	110
STANDARDS		112
	Two to tango	112
	The two boards' intellectual evolution	113
	The madness around probable	115
	A trusted global language worldwide	118
ANNUAL REPORTS		121
	Fun statements from annual reports	121
	Difficult FRC risk management	127
	Don't worry, HMRC is here to stay	130
	Deliberate distraction	131

	Worry about worrying	133
MAGAZINE ARTICLES		135
	Tweaking accountants	135
Chapter 4	**Surprising Fun**	**137**
JARGON		137
	Jargon is back	137
	Nothing standard about standard costing	138
STANDARDS		140
	The mysterious event in the past	140
	Rotten food	141
	A close member of the family	143
	Poetry, not only in standards	144
ANNUAL REPORTS		146
	Two ENTs	146
	Feet on the counter	148
	Odd peculiar risks in financial reports	149
	The irony of development	154
	Matter to emphasise	155
	BBB	158
MAGAZINE ARTICLES		160
	Superior British accountants	160
	To ding not dong financial results	162
FORMAL REPORTS		163
	Professional scepticism or deep suspicion	163
Chapter 5	**Bemused**	**167**
JARGON		167
	The ghosts of the tax gap	167
	Pretentious jargon	168
STANDARDS		170
	When is an accounting principle an assumption?	170
	The mysterious user of financial statements	171
	Are practical expedients practical?	173
	'As if' mixed with 'even if'	174
	Assets are invisible	175
ANNUAL REPORTS		177
	Hide it in the balance sheet	177
	Mostly 52, sometimes 53	178

	Really a risk?	180
	Bracing and chaos or general bloody-mindedness	184
	The not contingent non-liability	186
	How long does an aircraft fly?	187
Chapter 6	**The Most Boring Book in the World**	**190**
	The price of a transfer	190
	Comparing the potential	191
	Arms and thumbs	193
	Berries	193
	Poetry again	193
	Safe in the harbour	195
	Methods of transfer pricing	195
Chapter 7	**Reaching the Ridiculous**	**197**
	Revelation of company-specific risks	197
	Jargon construction	199
	My favourite	200
Annex 1	**Surprise Certificate**	**203**
Acknowledgements		**205**

Fun with Acronyms

Accountants swim in an alphabet soup of acronyms, contractions and abbreviations. They invent them whenever they can, on every subject possible. So this book is necessarily full of them. In itself, I can accept this, but this voracious appetite for the alphabet brings out three hoity-toity habits among the profession. In the first, they assume every non-accountant knows exactly what each set of capital letters means. In the book I have done the same, not, I hope, as a hoity-toity accountant, but to be concise and ensure unnecessary repetition. There are so many, I forget myself what some of them mean, and this list was invaluable while writing the book. In their second habit, they use the same letters to mean different things, but luckily for me their effect is often comical. Finally, they sometimes use the same initials chosen by other organisations.

ACCA	Association of Certified Chartered Accountants
ADS	American Depositary Share
AIA	Association of International Accountants
ASC	Accounting Standards Codification
BAU	business as usual
BBB	British Business Bank
BBF	British Business Finance
BBFSL	British Business Financial Services Ltd
BBI	British Business Investments
BBL	Bounce Back Loan
BEIS	Department for Business, Energy & Industrial Strategy (UK)
CAI	Institute of Chartered Accountants in Ireland
CCAB	Canadian Council for Aboriginal Business
CCAB	Catholic Charities of Boston
CCAB	Consultative Committee of Accountancy Bodies

CFO	Chief Financial Officer
CGU	Cash-Generating Unit
CIMA	Chartered Institute of Management Accountants
CIPFA	Chartered Institute of Public Finance and Accountancy
COSO	Committee of Sponsoring Organizations of the Treadway Commission
CPA	Institute of Certified Public Accountants in Ireland
CPA Australia	Certified Practising Accountants
CPA Canada	Chartered Professional Accountant
CPA Hong Kong	Certified Public Accountant
CPA India	Certified Public Accountant
CPA Ireland	Certified Public Accountant
CPA USA	Certified Public Accountant
CSM	Contractual Service Margin
CUP	Comparable Uncontrolled Price
DMCV	Direct Material Cost Variance
EBIT	earnings before interest and taxation
EBITDA	earnings before interest, taxation, depreciation and amortisation
EBITDAaL	earnings before interest, taxation, depreciation and amortisation after leases
EOM	emphasis of matter
EPS	earnings per share
FAF	Financial Accounting Foundation
FASB	Financial Accounting Standards Board
FD	Financial Director
FDA	Food and Drug Administration (in the USA)
FIFO	first in, first out
FRC	Financial Reporting Council
FRO	Future Ready Office
FVA	fair value approach
GAAP	Generally Accepted Accounting Practice (UK)
GAAP	Generally Accepted Accounting Principles (USA)

GLT	GSK Leadership Team
HMRC	His Majesty's Revenue and Customs
IAASA	Irish Auditing and Accounting Supervisory Authority
IAASB	International Auditing and Assurance Standards Board
IAS	International Accounting Standard
IASB	International Accounting Standards Board
ICAEW	Institute of Chartered Accountants in England and Wales
ICAI	Institute of Chartered Accountants of India
ICAS	Institute of Chartered Accountants in Scotland
IFRS	International Financial Reporting Standards
ISA	International Standards on Auditing
KAM	key auditing matter
KPI	key performance indicator
LIFO	last in, first out
MAP	mutual agreement procedure
MOU	Memorandum of Understanding
MURGC	material uncertainty relating to going concern
NASBA	National Association of State Boards of Accountancy (USA)
OECD	Organisation for Economic Co-operation and Development
PAB	Prescribed Accountancy Bodies (Ireland)
PBTCO	profit before tax from continuing operations
PCAOB	Public Company Accounting Oversight Board
RAB	Recognised Accountancy Bodies (Ireland)
RQB	Recognised Qualifying Bodies
RSB	Recognised Supervising Bodies
RSQ	revised standard quantity

SEC	Securities and Exchange Commission (USA)
SET	Senior executive team
TCFD	Task Force on Climate-related Financial Disclosures
UKEB	United Kingdom Endorsement Board
VFA	Variable Fee Approach
VOV	Variable Overhead Variance
WHO	World Health Organization

Fun with a Glossary

This glossary includes some of the accounting subjects covered in the book. I have not followed the recent trend of including in the glossary definitions that do not appear in the book.

Accountants
Accountants have two roles in life: 1) to present results in the best possible light; and 2) to ensure their company pays as little tax as possible (of course, legally).

Accounting standards
A collection of rules designed to restrict the imagination of accountants. Necessary because when no rules are in place, accountants go wild in their attempt to be reasonable.

Annual report
A compulsory document prepared annually by accountants to describe the brilliant work of top management throughout the year.

Assets
Items listed on a balance sheet, previously on the left, now at the beginning. Some are current, others non-current.

Auditor
Auditors are accountants who verify what other accountants do, which puts them in the category of extra dull, the dullest of the dull.

Benchmark
A limit set by auditors to measure materiality.

Critical Audit Matters
Same as a Key Audit Matters (see below) except auditors own up to their pessimism and worry by replacing 'key' with 'critical'.

Deferred taxation
An accounting trick not to report the exact amount of taxation payable. Instead, accountants calculate a theoretical amount payable (deferred tax liability) and a theoretical amount receivable (deferred tax asset), which is neither a receivable nor an asset.

Equity
Nothing to do with fairness or impartiality.

Estimated useful life
The number of years of service of an asset as estimated by accountants, always significantly lower than the real useful life of the asset.

Form 10K
A compulsory document, this one registered with the SEC, prepared annually by accountants in the USA to describe the brilliant work of top management throughout the year.

Form 20-F
Another compulsory document, registered with the SEC in the USA, prepared annually by accountants for foreign companies not following US GAAP to describe the brilliant work of top management throughout the year.

Forward-looking statement
A statement required by law in annual reports in the USA, which doesn't even look forward. It defines what the company thinks is a forward-looking statement, usually a projection into or a plan for the future. It then states that these projections or plans might not turn out as hoped by the company.

Going concern
Don't worry, the company will not go bankrupt in the next 12 months.

Goodwill
Excess paid above the true value when an entity purchases another, which accountants consider an asset, even though it represents poor negotiating skills.

Headroom
Not to be confused with overhead.

Key Audit Matters
Events that matter in an audit, same as Critical Audit Matters. 'Key' is used by optimistic auditors to convey confidence. It sounds more reassuring and less dangerous than 'critical', but it is not.

Liability
Accountants manage to classify payables and the value of a company in the same category. Some are long, others short.

Material
Accountants believe this word means both important and 'product in a factory', often when related to costing. Up to readers to determine which meaning is appropriate on their own; explanation never given.

Non-accountants
Accountants have an infallible technique for identifying a non-accountant. They wait for the question "What do you do?" And then gaze intensely into the eyes of their questioner and reply: "I am an accountant." When the light in the questioner's eyes goes out, they have found a non-accountant.

Overhead
Not to be confused with headroom or the rack on the train for suitcases.

Probable
Official accounting term which can have several meanings different to the English dictionary definition.

Residual value
An arbitrary value given to an asset by accountants, at the end of its arbitrary life.

Revenue recognition
An intellectual definition made by accountants to ensure non-accountants cannot guess what it means without asking. It simply means 'rules to define a sale'.

Risk statements
Padding put at the beginning of an annual report to make it boring to read, and to discourage readers from reaching the financial statements.

Sales
Now an obsolete accounting term, considered too vulgar and too 'working class', replaced by the word 'income' or increasingly by the more fashionable 'revenue'. (See also revenue recognition.)

Standard costing
Estimated costs invented by accountants; always different to actual costs.

Transfer pricing
Accounting transactions designed to confuse tax inspectors and optimise taxation.

Variance (in standards costing)
A failed attempt at a sophisticated name for the simple subtraction of two accounting numbers.

Write it down
If you say "Write it down" to an accountant, they do not pick up a pen ready to write; they think it is a question and they reply, "By how much?" Accountants have transformed the literal meaning into 'reduce the value', which they call written-down when completed, even if not in writing.

Introduction

I search for the silly in the serious. That is the essence of this book. As we all know, people consider accountancy to be, at best, dull and, at worst, really dull. Accountants rarely try to be anything other than serious and never deviate to the silly, at least never on purpose. And they would certainly never intentionally write anything amusing. But sometimes humour slips through the net, and I get my fun from these rare moments. I often have to go deep into the technical detail to find them. Sometimes, I don't even understand them myself, but even this can be a source of fun.

This book is for accountants by an accountant, albeit a retired one made a little odd and peculiar with age, but who feels, after all these years, that he's earned the right to have a little fun with the serious subject of accounting. For the non-accountants who understand annual reports and financial statements, I am happy if I bring on the start of a smile.

I tested some technical sections on my sister, who is a non-accountant and doesn't want to understand financial statements. She didn't smile. This is her beautiful reaction to one of my early versions on standard costing:

> Oh dear. I was lost on the first line. I vaguely wondered if standard was the same as average and it didn't make sense after that. Not that the definition would have helped. It wouldn't have. It did read to me like a handbook, which was trying to be friendly but the subject matter was too technical.

If you are in her category, the book will confirm what you always thought: accountants are complicated and dull! That may be, but if you are looking for ways to laugh at them or mock them, you might find something to go on, but only if you can get past that feeling of 'Oh dear'.

Seven accounting sisters
My first bit of fun comes from the structure of accounting in the UK. There are seven accounting organisations: two associations and five institutes. Six are chartered, one has no charter, another is both certified and chartered, three are country based, two concentrate on accounting specialities, five are accounting generalists, four have the authorisation to complete statutory audits in the UK, but only two can complete statutory audits in Ireland. Instead of designing one organisation to represent all accountants, they prefer seven with 31 different variations to ensure clarity. (Note: 31 is what the numbers add up too: 2+5+6 ... etc.)
Here are the seven:

ACCA	Association of Chartered Certified Accountants
AIA	Association of International Accountants
CAI	Institute of Chartered Accountants in Ireland [2]
CIMA	Chartered Institute of Management Accountants
CIPFA	Chartered Institute of Public Finance and Accountancy
ICAEW	Institute of Chartered Accountants in England and Wales
ICAS	Institute of Chartered Accountants in Scotland

You can see the keenness for 'Chartered'. Chartered here does not mean 'hired'. A 'hired accountant' would not be elegant and might suggest an association with looser morals. The reason for chartered is royalty. Queen Victoria and Queen Elizabeth granted royal charters to all accounting bodies but one. This gives chartered accountants a high moral status and still leaves those accountants who do not believe in kings and queens the choice of an institute not connected to royalty (a choice limited to one, but still a choice), the AIA.

I guess the seven accounting bodies realise how complicated this situation is. Tradition and history are holding them back from simplification. All attempts to merge one or two institutes have failed – and one can only guess at the reasons: egos, prestige (real or imagined), size, image. Which of the seven presidents would voluntarily give up their position? Reasons to keep the status quo are endless.

To explore ways in which the complicated landscape of accountancy might be simplified, and in an effort to show that they can work together, talk together, cooperate and coordinate, a committee was set up in 1974: the Consultative Committee of Accountancy Bodies (CCAB). But even here they failed: it would seem that the AIA was never invited to take part and the CIMA quit in 2011 because the committee talked too much about auditing. So then there were five – they consult but not all of them. How complicated is that?

And they don't talk about everything. The CCAB acts collectively, only to 'promote sustainable growth in the UK economy through the accountancy profession', but again only in 'two specific areas: tackling economic crime and promoting the value of the contribution of the accountancy profession to the UK economy'. They do not consult on common curriculums, common examinations, common values or any topic around rationalisation of the profession. 'We MUST remain separate, but let's talk together anyway.'

Now, this accounting CCAB is not to be confused with the other CCABs: one acts for Aboriginal people in Canada – the Canadian Council for Aboriginal Business – and the other for the Catholic Charities of Boston in the USA, without even mentioning the UK's only independent accreditation scheme for Clinical Animal Behaviourists (https://www.ccab.uk/).

In exasperation, no doubt, successive governments have stepped in to control this chaos. One such effort led to the setting up of a statutory body, the Financial Reporting Council (FRC). It does not have a mission but it does have a Purpose:

> "The FRC's Purpose is to serve the public interest by setting high standards of corporate governance, reporting and audit and by holding to account those responsible for delivering them."

'Those responsible for delivering them' must be the UK accounting profession, although it doesn't actually say so.

The FRC then invented and appointed some recognised bodies. The Recognised Qualifying Bodies (RQB) are five out of the seven: ACCA, AIA, CAI, ICAEW and ICAS. The Recognised Supervisory Bodies (RSB), which can carry out statutory audits, are only four: ACCA, CAI, ICAEW and ICAS. The AIA misses out on the supervisory role but is better off than the CIMA and the CIPFA, which miss out on both.

Do not bother trying to understand the distinction between an RQB and an RSB. Just acknowledge they are irrelevant for non-accountants, and too complicated for accountants who do not carry out audits. Auditors have to learn the distinction – their livelihood depends on it.

The Irish government did the same by setting up the Irish Auditing and Accounting Supervisory Authority (IAASA), similar to the FRC. They do not have a Purpose, but they do have a MISSION (their capitals not mine – it must be an important mission):

> "Upholding quality corporate reporting and an accountable profession."[1]

But take note, before their MISSION they have a VISION (their capitals again):

> "Public trust and confidence in quality auditing and accounting."[1]

And instead of RQBs and RSBs, they set up equivalents, calling them PABs (Prescribed Accountancy Bodies) and RABs (Recognised Accountancy Bodies).There are currently six PABs: ACCA, AIA, CIMA, CIPFA, CPA and CAI; but only three RABs: ACCA, CPA and CAI. Note that there is yet another accounting body in Ireland, not recognised in the UK: CPA, the Institute of Certified Public Accountants in Ireland.

But there was a revolution in Ireland in 2022, when the IAASA agreed to revoke the recognition of the Institute of Chartered Accountants in England and Wales (ICAEW) and the Institute of Chartered Accountants of Scotland (ICAS) at their request. They are no longer PABs or RABs. So now we have a curious situation where the ICAEW and the ICAS are not recognised in Ireland, but the CAI is recognised in the UK.

Amazing as it might seem, this chaotic organisation of the profession does work. Accountants don't see chaos, they see complexity.

And living with it is second nature to them. So much so, that they cannot see anything ridiculous in the way their profession is set up.

More choice, more confusion

This variety of institutes allows students to choose the type of accountant they wish to become, where a single institute would not. Accountants who wish to 'lead in business' should choose the Irish institute. Those who wish to be a 'force for change' should join the ICAEW. Accountants who like driving should join the ACCA or the CIMA. The ACCA not only 'drive change in the accounting sector' but their accountants 'have the strategic thinking, technical skills and professional values to drive their organisations forward' – a classic in bus and lorry imagery, copied by the CIMA, whose accountants also 'drive organisations forward'.

I am surprised more accountants do not join the Scottish institute 'to have a rewarding career in business and beyond'. 'Beyond' sounds almost mystical, which is odd for accountants. I am not sure what it means: beyond where or beyond what? Beyond Hadrian's Wall? The ICAS do boast that 14% of their members work outside Scotland. That must be it!

But the Scottish institute is not alone in promoting travel. In Ireland, they use the word 'global' to explain their diversity, as in 'global career recognition'. The Certified Accountants prefer 'all over the world', which is precise and clear. In England, their members work 'across 190 countries'. Now, I have worked in several countries, but I have never worked across them.

But, above all, the different accounting bodies compete for superlatives. In Scotland, accountants are on the 'fast track to unlock some of the most powerful and rewarding positions'. In England and Wales, they pursue 'the most interesting and rewarding opportunities'. In Ireland, they only have 'exciting career opportunities'. Accountants in the CIPFA 'enjoy working in public services and making a difference to society'. Not quite as excessive, the ACCA have 'the best and most interesting roles'.

The less ambitious should join the AIA. They merely 'boost their credibility' and help to achieve their 'professional goals', whatever they might be. Membership of CIMA would be the best fit for the seriously unambitious. They only claim their 'opportunities are as open-ended as you want them to be'.

I suppose this is what the accounting bodies call marketing. Make it lively with decision words – lead, drive, force –, add a few marvellous adjectives – rewarding, interesting, exciting – and finish with a couple of catchphrases.

But accountants never choose their profession for these lofty reasons. The key comes from the National Association of State Boards of Accountancy (NASBA) in the USA, who give the 'top five reasons to become a CPA' (a Certified Public Accountant) as:

1) Prestige and respect
2) Career development
3) Career security
4) Job satisfaction
5) Money and benefits

But, once qualified, young financial professionals in the USA, when asked what would inspire them most to become a Chief Financial Officer (CFO), choose money. Here is a summary of the results:

- 45% high salary
- 28% managing financial operations
- 25% working closely with a company's CEO to influence and make key business decisions
- 24% managing a team
- 25% problem solving [2]

The survey results add up to more than 100%. This could mean that these finance professionals choose the high salary first and then choose something (truly) inspirational, such as managing financial operations. On reflection, this inspiration is exclusive to accountants. Few people I know would find this inspiring.

You will have noticed these statistics and opinions are compiled from accountants in the USA. I am assuming that British and Irish accountants have broadly similar opinions to their colleagues in

America. I don't know if this is true. I couldn't find an equivalent survey in the UK or Ireland.

Conspirators

Outside the UK, accounting professions are more streamlined, but still find ways to confuse us. Several countries have conspired together to use the initials CPA to identify themselves. Here are six:

CPA USA	Certified Public Accountant
CPA Hong Kong	Certified Public Accountant
CPA India	Certified Public Accountant
CPA Ireland	Certified Public Accountant [3]
CPA Australia	Certified Practising Accountants
CPA Canada	Chartered Professional Accountant

These initials were not chosen by chance by the different accounting bodies. Accountants have a habit in their jargon of taking a word, or in this instance a set of initials, and giving them different meanings. CPA gives the impression they are the same, whereas accountants know they are not. As you can see, accountants like the letter C, echoing an allusion to royalty as in 'chartered' in the UK, but have to resort to 'certified' as a second best, except for the Canadians. They are more blatant and have chosen chartered without anything being granted by the King, who is still head of state in Canada. Cheeky!!

I don't know who copied whom with the choice of public and the letter P. Australian and Canadian accountants decided to be more imaginative with their 'practising' and 'professional' while staying in the CPA mould. However, they have all dropped using the full name and resort to the initials CPA, which is now a well-known and respectable equivalent to 'chartered', even if most people do not know what the C and P represent.

As another aside, the Institute of Chartered Accountants in Ireland (CAI) decided a long time ago not to include the initial 'I' for institute as part of its acronym, so in 1949 the Indians stepped in to confuse us with their more logical ICAI – Institute of Chartered Accountants in India. Take note: CAI is Irish, ICAI is Indian.

Disagreement on accounting standards

In addition to the chaotic situation in the UK and the calculated confusion of CPA in other countries, another structural anomaly makes life complicated for all. Accountants cannot agree on the rules for preparing financial statements of companies around the world. They call these rules 'accounting standards', and they have two separate 'boards' that make them up. One is in the USA: the Financial Accounting Standards Board (FASB). The other, based in London, covers more or less the rest of the world: the International Accounting Standards Board (IASB).

The IASB is part of the IFRS Foundation, which organises and publishes these international standards. They call the standards IFRS Standards. The foundation promotes the initials IFRS and uses them as their name and logo, such that on their website (https://www.ifrs.org/), you have to scroll right to the bottom to 'Trademarks' to find what the initials actually represent. They don't want us to know who they are. IFRS represents International Financial Reporting Standards. IFRS Standards then is International Financial Reporting Standards Standards. That, you have to agree, is repetitive and, to be kind, silly. So, not to distract us further, because I smile every time I see 'IFRS Standards', I refer nearly always to the IASB, rather than the IFRS, when I mention their standards.

The FASB belongs to the FAF (Financial Accounting Foundation), and they call their standards FASB Accounting Standards Codification. In full, this reads Financial Accounting Standards Board Accounting Standards Codification. So the FASB follow their IASB colleagues in repetition, this time with double repetition. One-upmanship? Let's leave them to their petty games.

Non-accountants assume that financial results published under the two standards are more or less the same. Accountants know they are not, but they never bother to explain the differences. They state their accounts are prepared under one standard or the other, and that, for them, is sufficient. They force users of financial statements to accept this anomaly.

Accountants actually write extensive explanations to help fellow members and students understand these anomalies, but they don't tell the general public. They argue, of course, that the information is available to anyone who reads accounting books and articles. But, as we all know, nobody reads accounting books and articles – except accountants. Some accountants themselves don't read accounting books and articles, so they don't know of these differences either, which is one of the reasons I reveal them here. I didn't even know some of them myself, until I compared the two accounting standards in detail.

But there are simple differences which the two boards could agree upon. Many of them are so minor that it becomes comical when they refuse to compromise. Take, for instance, the reduction in value of inventory, called 'inventory write-downs'. The FASB does not allow their reversal whereas the IASB does. Who cares about write-downs, let alone their reversal? Nobody, except for the two boards.

The two boards talked together for many years to try to agree on the same rules, but gave up and now only agree to disagree, while maintaining a semblance of consultation to show the outside world they cannot be considered obstinate. Again, the system works, but only because the two boards force their non-decisions on the financial world.

Sources of fun

As I have already said, I search for the silly in the serious. I find these 'once in a while' silly events in accounting literature: standards, textbooks, interviews, articles, annual reports, even financial statements. I go through long bouts of reading boredom to find them, but the gems they leave compensate for the time I spend.

Annual reports

I find annual reports a special source of fun. It might seem I concentrate my ire on a few pharmaceutical and grocery companies, while leaving out many others. In some ways this is true, because I have not yet reviewed other industries. I reviewed the 2021 and 2022 annual reports of eight pharmaceutical companies, four based in the USA (Abbott Laboratories, AbbVie Inc, Bristol-Myers Squibb Company, and Johnson & Johnson) and four based in Europe (AstraZeneca, GlaxoSmithKline (now known as GSK), Sanofi and Novartis). This arose when I decided to compare the risk statements of companies in the same industry to see if anything unusual came up. I chose the pharmaceutical industry as a place to start, and I chose these eight companies because they are well known. I found much to write about.

I then targeted the grocery industry and discovered not much to say. I read the annual reports of Costco Wholesale, Wm Morrisons Supermarkets, Tesco, Target Corporation, Walmart and Nestle, again for the years 2021 and 2022. Their annual reports are boring. I found only one common subject to write about and it is not part of the financial statements. There are, however, two exceptions: Associated British Foods and Unilever. Their annual reports are a delight to read, as you will see later.

I also read the annual reports of three government organisations: the FRC itself, His Majesty's Revenue and Customs (HMRC) and the British Business Bank (BBB). I had to search for the fun, but it's there.

I must emphasise, I am not picking on these companies. I have no gripes against their management or accountants. On the contrary, they should continue their practice of apparently copying last year's version and pasting it into the current year. This gives me something to write about. Nestle's and Walmart's annual reports, for example, I dislike. They should fire the person who checks their annual reports to take out the fun.

Risk statements

I dislike risk statements in annual reports because they tell us nothing we didn't know before reading them, so I take them apart with some pleasure.

Companies on both sides of the Atlantic are required to describe material risks threatening their business. The stated objective is to help potential investors decide whether to invest in the company and to help actual shareholders to assess the risk of their investment.

American companies list their risks in their annual reports, and in their formal submission to the SEC, called Form 10K in a compulsory section called Risk Factors, where they let the reader decide how relevant they are. British companies go further and boast about the process they call Risk Management. They insist, for instance, that the risk processes are *imbedded* into company procedures or that they carry out *robust assessments* of potential risks. They use risk buzz words, such as risk appetite and risk overview, to show their effectiveness. Sometimes they throw in trendy topics and convert them into risks, such as *climate risk*.

AstraZeneca, for instance, have a report they call 'Group Risk Report', which is reviewed by the Board to show how systematic and professional they are. Sometimes, companies prepare annual risk reports. The efficient companies prepare quarterly ones. They set up committees and councils with peculiar names to review their risks, for instance the ROCC in GSK, which stands for the Risk Oversight & Compliance Council, or the ARC, which means the Audit & Risk Committee. People are appointed to teach employees about risk. Risks have to be identified, monitored, evaluated, graded, audited, communicated, approved and then written into the annual report. It is all so perfect.

Risk statements are so dull, dry and long, I doubt if anyone ever reads them. For instance, risk factors in the Abbott Laboratories annual report run for six pages and over 4,300 words. Bristol Myers Squibb either do a better job of describing their risks or have a high-risk company, because their Risk Factor section has over 10,500 words.

Whether one has to plough through 4,000 or 10,000 words to understand a company's risk profile, reading them is a daunting task. Companies do try to help by separating them into sub-sections with headings such as Operating Risks, Business Risks, Legal Risks and sometimes even General Risks. But this gives us no clarity, because so many of the risks are the same from company to company. This means company-specific risks are lost in this mountain of information. I suspect they do this on purpose.

Jargon

I had a field day with accounting jargon, especially jargon I had never heard of. I found most of the best examples of jargon by chance. They spring out of dull financial text and make me smile. Accountants, for instance, have a habit of taking ordinary words and turning them into accounting jargon with a different meaning. Sometimes, these words are accepted by accountants worldwide, while others stay at the company or country level. Accountants who work in these companies use their company-specific jargon so often that they include them in their annual reports as though they are recognised everywhere. These are the ones I have the most fun with.

Other sources

I found unusual articles about accountants in the *Wall Street Journal*, *The Economist* and *accountingWEB* which contribute to the book. I also comment on the activities of two recently formed UK government organisations – the British Business Bank and the United Kingdom Endorsement Board – as well as the staid His Majesty's Revenue and Customs in their dealings with taxation. The International Auditing and Assurance Standards Board managed to make me laugh, so they get a couple of mentions too.

Why the chapter headings?

I decided to classify each article in the book into one of five levels of fun. I arbitrarily declare these to be: Entertaining Fun, Silly Fun, Amusing Fun, Surprising Fun and Bemused and these are the titles of the first five chapters. As an illustration, I have written two articles on the subject of what accountants call 'material'. I find the way the IASB defines the word entertaining, given the time and effort they put into it, so it goes into Chapter 1 Entertaining Fun. However, the two accounting standards boards tried, without success, to agree on a common definition for the term 'material'. This, I consider quite silly, even amusing. I put the article into Chapter 2 Silly Fun even if could also have gone into Chapter 3 Amusing Fun.

Everyone admits humour is personal and subjective, so this classification is mine alone. And not everyone agrees. For instance, some accountants, in my test phase, asked me for solutions to my supposed criticisms on 'going concern' and 'standard costing'. I sensed annoyance, even anger, at my attempts of humour on these serious subjects. I don't have solutions and I am not criticising. I just have fun writing about them. Many of the subjects made me smile when I found them. I give the one that made me laugh the loudest a special place on its own in the last chapter, but whoever wrote the original will never accept my classification of it as the funniest event in the book.

[1] Have a look here: https://iaasa.ie/about/. Note also their striving and regulating VALUES, to complete their MISSION and VISION.

[2] CPA Practice Advisor, 70% of Young Finance Pros Choose Big Firms to Fast-Track Career, 29th September 2021, https://www.cpapracticeadvisor.com/accounting-audit/news/21240291/70-of-young-finance-pros-choose-big-firms-to-fasttrack-career.

[3] Early in 2024, CPA Ireland entered into talks to merge with Chartered Accountants Ireland, or to use their word: amalgamate. It will be interesting to see what they decide on as a name after the amalgamation. Could it be Chartered Public Accountants, CPA, as in Canada?

Chapter 1

Entertaining Fun

JARGON
The bearer plant

What is a 'bearer plant'? Flowers delivered by a florist? No, accountants don't use the word 'plant' in the sense of a flower or a bush. They use it in the phrase 'property, plant and equipment'. There is even a standard – IAS 16, Property, Plant and Equipment – to explain what it is all about. Plant for an accountant is a generic word for machinery used in a factory.

The word 'bearer' for an accountant means: 'If you hold it in your hand, you own it.' It is something in one's possession, such as bearer shares or bearer bonds that are not officially registered.

So, logically, one would assume that the expression 'bearer plant' would be a piece of machinery that a person could carry around with them, as opposed to machinery that is too heavy or fixed in place. Under this definition, a computer could be a bearer plant, but not a bus.

BUT NO!

A bearer plant, for an accountant, is a living plant. [1]

Why did the IASB not call their bearer plant a living plant and move on? Are they intentionally being misleading? Or are they having a little fun?

But the bearer plant is not any plant; it must have the same characteristics as a fixed asset. It has to bear fruit (thus the word 'bearer') for more than one year and it cannot be for sale – only its fruit is for sale. A walnut tree, for instance, is a bearer plant.

But then an ordinary person doesn't call a tree a plant, they call it a tree. Only accountants call it a plant.

[1] Paragraph 6 of International Accounting Standard 16 Property, Plant and Equipment (IAS 16): 'A bearer plant is a living plant ...'

Where is concern going?

'Going concern' – what an odd expression accountants have invented. Where is concern going? Or perhaps how is concern going? As in 'the going is good'? It cannot be a farewell, as in going away. Concerns don't go anywhere. And is concern a worry? No, concern here is nothing to worry about, even though accountants worry about concern when 'going' is attached. Nor is it related to the phrase 'to whom it may concern'. Concern here means organisation or enterprise. That I suppose is obvious for an accountant but not for the ordinary person. Why didn't they call it a 'leaving worry'? That is just as understandable.

The French call it 'continuité d'exploitation', which translated literally means 'continuity in trading'. French accountants try to make their term clear from the outset. English-speaking accountants make it difficult to understand by giving it this unusual name.

There is even some doubt whether the term was invented by an accountant. It seems that the first reference appeared as an advertisement a little over 200 years ago, when a bottle factory was put up for sale.[1] Did the owner place the advert with the offending phrase or did he ask his accountant to sell the factory? It's a mystery! If they didn't invent it, accountants have certainly taken it over and created the monster it has become for the auditing profession.

Accountants struggle to define 'going concern'. Is it a concept, a principle, a standard, an assumption, a basis, a focus, an assessment or an accounting term? Perhaps they believe it's all eight.

Going concern is not a standard, but sometimes accountants get themselves into a twist and declare it to be one. An example comes in the heading of a statement explaining guidance issued by the FASB:

"What FASB's Going Concern Standard Really Means For Your Company."[2]

And then in the very first sentence, the article states that going concern is an assumption. I don't believe that such errors arise from the accountants' nature to make things complicated, but they do add to the confusion.

Going concern is an assumption in many accounting documents and this is their favourite term. But the accounting firm KPMG choose to be different, and declare that going concern is a presumption:

> "The going concern presumption – i.e. that the company will be able to meet its obligations when they become due – is fundamental to financial reporting." [3]

I guess they wanted to add one more word to the eight already used by accountants. To be pernickety, this choice must be related to the difference in meaning between 'presumption' and 'assumption'. So let's see what is involved! Not much. Most dictionaries give the same meaning: 'to take for granted'. So KPMG complicate our lives further by choosing presumption. No, you will say, presumption is a little more assertive than assumption, so not quite the same.

None of the accounting institutes or accounting boards admits going concern is a principle, yet some organisations elevate the term to one. I find Wikipedia give us the best example. They throw in this sentence under the heading *Accounting* in their odd peculiar explication of going concern:

> "The going concern principle allows the company to defer some of its prepaid expenses until future accounting periods." [4]

A few business schools declare that going concern is a principle, as well as several accounting blogs written by qualified accountants, accounting software companies, accountancy training organisations and many others. This adds to the general confusion around its definition, which accountants do nothing to correct.

The IFRS are alone in calling going concern a focus in the heading of their document, 'Going concern—a focus on disclosure', published in January 2021. Whereas the ICAEW go out of their way not to call going concern anything. And they succeed most of the time by using this trick:

> "Accounts are usually prepared on the **basis** that the business is a 'going concern'." [5]

This way they do not fall into the trap of writing 'going concern basis', which others use. But they fail miserably in their document entitled 'The Going Concern Hub: where to start'. [6] Here, in the title, they call going concern a 'hub', and then in the first paragraph of the document, they call going concern a 'fundamental bedrock'. This increases the number of ways of qualifying going concern from eight to 11.

However, the champions when it comes to describing going concern are the ACCA, who manage, in the space of a few words, to make it three things at once in their statement:

> "The concept of going concern
> An entity prepares financial statements on a going concern basis when, under the going concern assumption …" [7]

In 21 words, going concern is a concept, a basis and an assumption. All three! How about that? They are true believers in what I have come to call the going concern trinity: the concept, the basis and the holy assumption. Going concern is a concept, they say, when it's theorised, a basis when it's applied, and an assumption when preparing financial statements. So there you are, three is okay but not 11.

But if I give the impression that this rambling jumble proves the nonsense of it all, you can rest assured that accounting experts have none of it. To them, this confusion makes perfect sense.

[1] Source: *Oxford English Dictionary*: '1818 Caledonian Mercury 27 Apr. (advt.) The Bottle Manufactory is a going concern which would be a great advantage to a purchaser, in the view of continuing the business.'
[2] Source: https://anderscpa.com/what-fasbs-going-concern-standard-really-means-for-your-company.
[3] Source: KPMG's use of going concern as a presumption: https://advisory.kpmg.us/articles/2020/going-concern.html.

[4] Source: https://en.wikipedia.org/wiki/Going_concern, Version May 2022.
[5] Source: https://www.icaew.com/-/media/corporate/files/about-icaew/press-release-documents/covid-19-going-concern-guidance-for-small-businesses.ashx
[6] Source: https://www.icaew.com/insights/viewpoints-on-the-news/2020/june-2020/the-going-concern-hub-where-to-start.
[7] Source: https://www.accaglobal.com/gb/en/student/exam-support-resources/fundamentals-exams-study-resources/f8/technical-articles/going-concern.html.

Not only fair but also true

In the opinion of auditors the world over, financial statements are declared to be true and fair. 'True and fair' has become such a common expression that no-one thinks about it anymore. It trips effortlessly off the tongue like 'fair and square'.

But why are financial statements both true and fair?

True on its own would be fine. True is strong, and associated with many affirmative adjectives: authentic, correct, genuine, right, valid, accurate, exact, etc., etc. Fair has a connotation of honesty and being in accordance with the rules. Even on its own, it would be acceptable. But if I had to choose, I prefer true financial results over fair.

There must be an important reason for them having to be both fair and true at the same time. Is it possible, for instance, that some financial statements could be true but not fair and vice versa? If they are true, who cares if they might also be unfair! Many things are unfair, if true, but not financial statements. How could they be unfair, if they are true?

It might be possible, in theory, because of degree, that they be fair but not true. But what intellectual contortions would be necessary for an accountant to prepare three sets of financial statements, one set that is true, another that is fair, and yet another that is both true and fair? What change in the numbers would be necessary? I suspect none. All three would be identical.

What, then, is the ruse auditors play on us by stressing that their financial statements are both true and fair? They don't tell us.

Only fair

Auditors in the USA report differently. They 'present fairly' the financial statements. In other countries, they use either 'true and fair' or 'present fairly'. For instance KPMG, the auditors of the state railway company in Italy, Ferrovie dello Stato Italiane, in the English version of their audit report use the expression 'true and fair view'. The Italian version is a little different: *una rappresentazione veritiera e corretta*, which literally means true and correct. But the origin is clear.

You probably don't know and don't care, but accountants have spent time and energy examining the difference between 'presents fairly' and 'true and fair' in their audit reports.

Are, for instance, financial statements in the UK more accurate than those in the USA because they are not only fair but also true? Using simple English, this must be true. Both are fair but only one is true. And what extra work do auditors do to make the additional claim of true? None.

To show I am not making this up, in June 2014 the Financial Reporting Council wrote in a paper headed 'True and Fair':

"Fair presentation under IFRS is equivalent to a true and fair view."

So in practice there is no difference between the two terms. Yet another ruse accountants play on users of financial statements.

The origin of the ruse arises from the United Kingdom Companies Act of 1948, which put the 'true and fair' concept into law, but never defined 'truth' and 'fairness' in accounting terms. Accounting intellectuals have been trying to define them ever since. Many countries that prepare financial statements under IFRS also decided on the true and fair concept, even if they don't really know what it means, because there is no definition. And to complete the trick, the Americans decided on their 'presents fairly'.

We now have two opposing camps saying different things that mean the same. I would have thought this would be the subject of discussion between the two accounting bodies. Let's be clear and transparent instead of confusing. But of course it is not. And never will be, ever. They want to keep the ruse alive!

Serious research in New Zealand [1] has shown, for instance, that most people prefer 'true and fair' to 'presents fairly'. Now I'm not sure how necessary that was. Any logical person, who was asked whether true and fair was better than fair on its own, would surely choose the phrase with both.

Not only do they prefer true and fair, but the research [1] reveals that many people believe the two phrases have different meanings. This too is logical. If the same audit firm in the UK states that financial statements are true and fair, but states that another set of financial statements in USA only presents fairly [2] the results, any logical person would believe that one is truer than the other.

But they are, as accountants say, 'equivalent', or, in simple language, the same, despite one stating true, and the other not. For accountants, fair on its own means the same as true and fair. How's that for clarity and logic?

[1] 'True and fair view' versus 'present fairly in conformity with generally accepted accounting principles', N. E. Kirk, Discussion Paper Series 208, August 2001, Massey University, School of Accountancy, copyright – 2001 N. E. Kirk, Massey University.

[2] Bear with me, accountants recognise this strange word order: 'presents fairly the results'. They use it all the time in audit reports, and to them it sounds fluent and accurate. Everyone else, i.e. normal people, would say 'presents the results fairly', which clearly flows more naturally. What accountants are trying to tell us is that the presentation is fair, not the results, and yet what we all hope for is fair results.

Accounting headroom

I had always thought headroom was the space between the top of my head and the roof of my car. However, I recently discovered 'headroom' in the 2022 annual report of Associated British Foods. They can't be measuring the height of the ceiling in their head office. So perhaps their accountants use the second more figurative meaning of headroom: 'freedom of action'.

But no, it has a value: "Headroom was $232m on a CGU carrying value of $1,003m."

To me, this statement means nothing. Now, naturally, I have taken it out of context and thrown it into my article for effect. But, believe me, even in context I have no idea what it means. To help, CGU is a cash-generating unit, and the context is impairment testing and judgements made by management.

Here is another one giving even less insight:

> "Each of the Group's CGUs had headroom under the annual impairment review."

Reading this, I would guess that when accountants do their impairment tests, the future cash flows exceed the carrying value, and this excess could be headroom. If so, my assumption above is incorrect. Accounting headroom has nothing to do with freedom of action, as I thought, but is closer to the space between the top of my head and the roof of my car.

Accountants writing the annual report of Associated British Foods mention 'headroom' 14 times in 2021 and another 16 times in 2022. They measure headroom in many accounting issues: goodwill and intangible assets, but also in the appreciation of going concern and, surprisingly, in the company's liquidity risk. Headroom has become versatile and a part of the accounting environment in Associated British Foods.

I looked around for more 'headrooms' in other annual reports. I only found it again in the 2022 annual report of bp. (Note if you didn't know: British Petroleum changed their name to BP p.l.c. in 2001, and I guess as a style choice or marketing gimmick forget the capitals in other documents.) Here it is:

> "The increase in headroom for both segments relates to movements due to the passage of time and price impacts."

So, in bp, headroom has value too.

From the initiative of these two British companies, accountants might decide to unleash headroom into the public domain as a piece of recognised, much-loved accounting jargon. It would certainly contribute to enlivening the rather austere vocabulary we use. But for the moment, headroom remains colloquial and unknown. It still makes me smile.

Why make deferred taxes so complicated?

A tax liability represents an amount you owe to the tax man. Accountants, though, believe that taxation for companies is more complicated, so they invented deferred taxation. This is a simple concept, but they made its calculation excessively complex by adding a multitude of technical terms to make it work, according to them, more effectively.

A tax liability in the balance sheet is rarely, if ever, what the company owes to tax authorities. Most of the time, it is much more and, theoretically, payable over several years. And a tax asset is never an overpayment of taxes.

Accountants call the two basic technical terms, upon which they base the concept, permanent differences and timing differences. I suppose they had to call them something, but they choose terms that are deliberately misleading. A permanent difference, for instance, is not a difference but simply no tax payable – zero. One could argue that it is permanent because no tax is ever due, but it isn't a difference.

A timing difference represents tax payable later, so 'timing' here seems reasonable, but it is not a difference either but a delay. And then, to make it all the more difficult, they break down timing differences into two: 'taxable temporary differences' and 'deductible temporary differences'.

As a reader of financial reports, you should know the precise meaning of these two terms, but I won't even bother to try to explain their definitions. It would be like splitting hairs when all you have is a brush. And anyway, who cares except the experts? Unfortunately, these terms appear often in financial reports and most reasonable shareholders don't understand what they mean. They assume that the people who prepare the financial statements understand what they write about and don't need to explain anything.

But I am not alone in believing that deferred taxation is complex – accountants admit it themselves. The ACCA in their explication of deferred taxes write:

> "All this terminology can be rather overwhelming and difficult to understand ..." [1]

Overwhelming is the word.

[1] The Association of Chartered Certified Accountants, Deferred Taxes, https://www.accaglobal.com/in/en/student/exam-support-resources/professional-exams-study-resources/strategic-business-reporting/technical-articles/deferred-tax.html.

STANDARDS
Refined material

'Material' to an accountant means important. The IASB believed their definition of 'material' was too imprecise. I can see nothing wrong with it, but I am not an expert. However, let's imagine the collective concern of the IASB over its apparent weakness. They must have had meetings to discuss what parts of the definition needed changing to improve it.

Here is the imprecise version that needs changing, obviously quite inadequate:

> "Omissions or misstatements of items are material if they could individually or collectively influence the economic decisions that users make on the basis of financial statements."

From the start, they decided not to invent something completely new. This definition needs some minor modifications, they thought. We must add three words, substitute one with a woolly phrase and eliminate another. I should note here that the process took two years, and the IASB formally consulted the accounting profession to make sure their decisions were acceptable.

Addition of word number one

The IASB believed the words 'omissions' and 'misstatements' in the definition did not explain the term 'material' enough. They thought there was a word missing and this word, would you believe, was 'obscuring'. Obscuring means aggregation and disaggregation – a complicated notion. It can also mean hiding something material in a mountain of immaterial information. This I can understand. I call it fraud. The discussions around deciding whether to add this word or leave it out must have been enlightening. It is a pity they did not reveal them.

The ICAEW, however, didn't seem to like the word 'obscuring' and they recommended in their representation that the IASB should give more explanations. The IASB ignored them.

Substitution of a word with a phrase

The IASB decided to change the word 'could'. 'Could' on its own is insufficient, too precise, they thought. They decided to bring in the Clapham omnibus and something more reasonable.

I will now digress to tell you the story of the omnibus. It explains why the IASB made this change, and anyway, I like the story so much, I have to tell it to you. I would never have thought a Clapham bus had any connection to financial statements, but there are two; one relates to the meaning of 'reasonable' and the other to the user of financial statements.

In 1903, Sir Richard Henn Collins MR, in his judgment in McQuire v Western Morning News [1903], wrote about fair comment where he defined the 'ordinary reasonable man' as 'the man on the Clapham omnibus'. Fair comment has evolved over time in various legal cases and, since then, the man on this particular bus has made many appearances in various court cases, and his opinion is now the gold standard in the definition of 'reasonable'.

The man has travelled far and wide, certainly much further than Clapham – and who could blame him? He is now known as 'the man on the Bondi train' [1] in Sydney and 'the man on the Bourke Street tram' [2] in Melbourne. He has also travelled to Hong Kong, where he is known as 'the man on the Shaukiwan tram'. [3]

But today 'he' could also be a woman. Where would the man and the ordinary reasonable woman go today? Let's suppose they travel together. They might be on a train to Brighton, or a Ryanair flight via Alicante to Benidorm. The train to Glasgow would, I think, be too expensive. And they would never be on a transatlantic flight to San Francisco. They might take a taxi from Leicester Square to Brixton, but certainly not to Kensington High Street or Sloane Square. They might drive to Clapham in their car. But what model would it be? Not a Ferrari or a Rolls, perhaps a Ford Fiesta or a Vauxhall Corsa, the two bestselling second-hand cars in the UK in 2023.

I think, though, they might no longer take the bus; the Underground would be quicker. But to which Clapham? The Northern line has three: Clapham Common, Clapham North and Clapham South. Or would they take the London Overground and get off at Clapham High Street or Clapham Junction? I suspect speed is not the issue. Anyway, Camden might be more representative today than Clapham. House prices are too expensive there.

The next time I am in London, I will take the 88 bus to Clapham High Street early in the afternoon to see if I can find him, and look out for her, especially as the last stop of the 88 bus route is still Omnibus Clapham. It would be fun to hear whether they still have the same opinion on 'could reasonably be expected', as back in 1903.

Back to the IASB. They decided to replace the word 'could' with 'could reasonably be expected to'. Their headquarters is, after all, in London, so everyone knows of Clapham, and some of their employees may even have taken the number 88 bus.

They chose this now legal expression over the more specific 'could'. But this, they realised, created a problem with the word 'users' in their definition. As soon as they included 'reasonable', the user of financial statements became the man on the Clapham omnibus. And he or now she, they decided, does not have an adequate financial education, and doesn't even know the concept of materiality. This is why they had to add word number two to their definition.

Addition of word number two
The board added the word 'primary' to 'users', giving us 'primary users'. So materiality now concerns ONLY primary users of financial statements. But having added primary, they needed to define it, which they kindly did:

> "... primary users are existing and potential investors, lenders and other creditors—those users who cannot require entities to provide information directly to them and must rely on general purpose financial statements for much of the financial information they need."

So they are investors, lenders and creditors. But the important word here, according to IFRS Practice Statement 2 is 'potential'. And 'potential' means, more or less, anyone. Further, all three groups should not be taken together. Each group of investors, lenders and creditors should be considered separately when deciding whether something is material or not. How's that for becoming tangled up in detail?

So, in order to see things through the eyes of primary users, accountants preparing financial statements and the auditors have to imagine they are investors, lenders or creditors. Imagine doing this three times, once for each group: considering, as if they were one of them, the decisions they might make, and then assessing whether they need to add information to the financial statements that could reasonably influence these theoretical users. Quite a feat of creativity for an accountant or auditor. They have to imagine they are in the others' heads and act out the part, before they prepare or audit the financial statements each year.

Addition of words number three and four

The term 'financial statements' needed to be qualified too, the Board thought. They have now become 'general purpose' financial statements. But no company ever mentions the term 'general purpose' in their annual reports. Audit reports should read, 'We have examined the general purpose financial statements …' but they don't. They prepare financial statements or annual financial statements, but never general purpose ones. So who decides if they are general purpose? It's a matter of professional judgement, no doubt, but whose judgement exactly? The preparer, the primary user, the auditor, or the judge at the trial in the event that someone in the future disagrees with the term 'general purpose', and goes to court?

Elimination of a word

Economic, as in 'economic decisions', was too specific said the IASB. They replaced it with the phrase 'influence the decisions'. Previously it was 'influence the economic decisions'. So now all decisions, and not only economic decisions, must be taken into account when assessing materiality. It is a pity they do not give us examples, because it is difficult to imagine what these decisions might be. Some investor, somewhere, must have made a non-economic decision after reading a material misstatement in some financial statements without obtaining compensation.

With these changes the new IASB definition of 'material', which came into effect on 1 January 2020, is as follows:

> "Information is material if omitting, misstating or obscuring it could reasonably be expected to influence the decisions that the primary users of general purpose financial statements make on the basis of those financial statements, which provide financial information about a specific reporting entity."

But does this new definition help accountants make materiality judgements in the preparation of financial statements? The IASB believe so. And of course we all do, because of the Clapham omnibus.

[1] Asprey, Michèle M. (2010) [2003], Plain Language for Lawyers, Federation Press, p. 119, ISBN 978-1-86287-775-7.

[2] Re Sortirios Pandos and Commonwealth of Australia [1991] AATA 18.

[3] SFAT (2009), Ng Chiu Mui v Securities and Futures Commission Application No 7 of 2007 (15 May 2009) (PDF), Securities and Futures Appeals Tribunal, p. 30.

Tied up in knots

As a jargon technique, the IASB choose a word, then stick it onto another to invent a new accounting term. The writers of IFRS 11 [1] chose 'joint' from the well-known accounting term 'joint venture' and invented five new accounting terms. Here is what they think of a joint venture:

> "A joint arrangement is either a joint operation or a joint venture." [2]

To define joint arrangement more precisely, they came up with joint control:

> "Joint control is the contractually agreed sharing of control of an arrangement ..." i.e. a joint arrangement.

With these three, they concocted a 'joint operator' and 'joint venturer' to make up the total of five.

Here they are:

> Joint arrangement
> Joint control
> Joint venture
> Joint operator
> Joint venturer

I am surprised that they did not include a joint controller, as being the person who prepares the contracts for joint control, whose definition would be simple:

> "A joint controller prepares contracts for joint controls."

And imagine my disappointment when, instead of inventing joint arranger, they fall back on the mundane 'party to a joint arrangement'. Perhaps they thought that seven new accounting terms would be excessive.

Even with these five, the writers of the standard sometimes get confused, and repetition can make sentences difficult to understand. Here is an example:

> "A party that participates in, but does not have joint control of, a joint operation might obtain joint control of the joint operation in which the activity of the joint operation constitutes a business as defined in IFRS 3." [3]

Clear as mud! Two joint controls and three joint operations in 38 words, nearly 30% of the words in the sentence.

Given this confusion, I had a look at what the FASB do in the USA for the same issue. Instead of inventing five accounting terms, they remain sober and limit their use to the two well-known 'joint' terms: joint venture and joint control. They don't use joint operators, joint arrangements or joint controllers. Instead, they invent two others, hitherto unknown in IFRS. The first is 'joint activity' to be used in fundraising, and the second is 'joint cost' to be used with joint activity.

As you can see, accountants are fond of joints.

But this is not the first time the IASB use this repetitive jargon technique. In IAS 21 [4] they combine three terms: 'foreign currency', 'functional currency' and 'presentation currency'. They then develop the technique in IFRS 7 [5] with the word 'risk', building on the well-known credit risk, but only daring to add four: 'currency risk', 'liquidity risk', 'interest rate risk' and 'market risk'. But they compensate their prudence by going wild with an elaborate 'credit risk rating grades', turning credit risk into an adjective.

With these repetitive accounting terms, IASB do manage to avoid getting tied up in knots. Only in IFRS 11 do they get tied up in joints.

[1] International Financial Reporting Standard 11 Joint Arrangements, IFRS 11.

[2] Paragraph 6 of International Financial Reporting Standard 11 Joint Arrangements, IFRS 11.

[3] Paragraph B33CA of International Financial Reporting Standard 11 Joint Arrangements, IFRS 11.

[4] International Accounting Standard 21 The Effects of Changes in Foreign Exchange Rates, IAS 21.

[5] International Financial Reporting Standard 7 Financial Instruments: Disclosures, IFRS 7.

The noble concept of the spectrum of inherent risk

The 'concept of the spectrum of inherent risk': [1] I wonder what this pompous concept could be. I first thought it related to risk management. But, no, auditors use this concept only in relation to possible misstatements in financial statements. It must, therefore, be a simple concept to understand. Or so I thought. But I was wrong.

Let's take, as a start, the definition of an inherent risk. In paragraph 4 of ISA 315, I found this:

"Inherent risk is described as the susceptibility of an assertion ..." [2]

So an inherent risk is not a risk. ISA 315 has turned it into 'the susceptibility of an assertion', whatever that might be. In the event that you think I am exaggerating and taking it out of context, I have put the whole definition below. [2] And I had thought that an inherent risk was a risk associated with the company involving a high degree of uncertainty, which could lead to material misstatement.

But to be fair to ISA 315, Appendix 2 gives us examples of inherent risk factors that could lead to these misstatements. There are five that auditors must consider: complexity, subjectivity, change, uncertainty and the susceptibility of management. Very helpful indeed.

Spectrum is defined in several complicated paragraphs. It depends on the auditor's 'professional judgment within a range, from lower to higher'. As you can see, the word 'spectrum' becomes 'range'. The word 'range' would have been less pompous than spectrum, and easier to understand. Yet this is the simple part of the explanation.

Auditors are then required to review a long list of possibilities, but don't worry, they are experts and know how to tackle the nature, size and complexity of the entity, inherent risk factors, the possibility that a misstatement may occur, the qualitative and quantitative aspects of the possible misstatement, and, the most important, 'assessed likelihood and magnitude of the misstatement'. By this time, any ordinary person is bored, and any auditor overwhelmed by the magnitude of their task. But it is not over yet.

Two paragraphs are devoted to the relationship between likelihood and magnitude, with, for instance, this profound example:

> "Rather, it is the intersection of the magnitude and likelihood of the material misstatement on the spectrum of inherent risk that will determine whether the assessed inherent risk is higher or lower on the spectrum of inherent risk."

That was helpful!

Finally, range is not relevant anyway. Auditors are only interested in the inherent risks 'close to the upper end of the spectrum of inherent risk'. This is what the IAS consider a significant risk: an identified risk that could lead to material misstatement. The low and medium risks are irrelevant as they do not lead to material misstatements. So, finally, it is not the spectrum that is important, only the upper range risks or the upper range susceptibilities of an assertion, to use the standard's wording.

You can imagine how reassured I was when I read the remarks of Tom Seidenstein of the International Auditing and Assurance Standards Board:

> "The revised standard (ISA 315) introduces new concepts to help auditors in identification and assessment of risk." [3]

He appears to believe the standard helps. But imagine how worried I became when he added 'including more consistent use of language'. They have been admirably consistent, but only in using inconsistent language.

Consistent is not the right word. He should have used entertaining. Even better, incomprehensible. Good luck to the auditors in their quest to apply the concept of the spectrum of inherent risk, or, as they explain, the 'concept of the range of susceptibility of an assertion'!

[1] International Standard on Auditing 315, ISA 315, (Revised 2019), Identifying and Assessing the Risks of Material Misstatement.

[2] Inherent risk is described as the susceptibility of an assertion about a class of transaction, account balance or disclosure to a misstatement that could be material, either individually or when aggregated with other misstatements, before consideration of any related controls.

[3] Taken from the remarks of Tom Seidenstein, Chair, International Auditing and Assurance Standards Board in his speech entitled 'The Future of International Standard-Setting' to the Institute of Chartered Accountants of England and Wales's audit conference 'Reflect, Reform, Refocus' in October 2019.

The confusion around GAAP

American accountants have to learn their accounting principles known as GAAP – Generally Accepted Accounting Principles – which are part of the rules set by the FASB.

'Generally accepted' is an odd expression to use. Why only generally? Could this mean that some people, some of the time, do not accept some of the principles? What, I wonder, are the parts that are not accepted, and who are the people who do not accept them?

I suspect that 'generally' here means 'definitely'. In which case, DAAP, as in Definitely Accepted Accounting Principles, or TAAP, as in Totally Accepted Accounting Principles, would be more accurate. Even just AAP, Accepted Accounting Principles, would be better. The mystery, however, remains unsolved, because American accountants never discuss this anomaly. The word 'generally' in this context has become so familiar, it now means fully accepted, not generally accepted.

The UK has their GAAP too, but it means something completely different. They do not have principles but a practice: Generally Accepted Accounting Practice. This is so familiar to UK accountants that they don't need to explain what the letters mean. And UK accountants follow their US colleagues and omit to explain why they use the term 'generally accepted'.

To use the explanation of the Institute of Chartered Accountants in England and Wales, UK GAAP 'is the body of accounting standards published by the UK's Financial Reporting Council (FRC).' These standards are in turn based on EU-adopted IFRS. Perhaps American accountants are more principled than the British ones, and the British practise the practical more than Americans.

So we have two GAAPs in two countries with different meanings. Non-accountants might find this confusing, but accountants in both countries don't care. They know what their particular GAAP means, and that is all that matters. They don't talk to each other anyway. The difference between the principle GAAP in the USA and the practice GAAP in the UK must simply be due to the gap in the Atlantic Ocean.

And I smile each time I step off the Underground in London, and hear the warning announcement, 'Mind the gap'. Which one, I wonder? We now have three.

ANNUAL REPORTS
Looking forward in a statement
Nobody ever reads the 'Cautionary Statement Regarding Forward-Looking Statements' in annual reports. So I have taken up the noble and committed cause, becoming the first person to ever dare enter this

mysterious territory. I have read a few of these statements so that you don't have to.

The law requires companies to make these cautionary statements, but there is no consensus on which law applies. The wisest companies don't include any reference to the source. A few try to be as complete as possible, with a list such as this:

> "... within the meaning of Section 27A of the Securities Act of 1933, as amended, Section 21E of the Securities Exchange Act of 1934, as amended (the 'Exchange Act'), and the United States Private Securities Litigation Reform Act of 1995, as amended." [1]

I found one that mentions the two sections 27A and 21E of what they call the 'Exchange Act' without dates. They say nothing of the 1995 Reform Act cited above. And I found one with this Reform Act only and no reference to any other.

Either companies are unsure which law to reference or they are opting for the wisdom of ambiguity. Who cares anyway? They all, without exception, have a cautionary statement, so at least one law must apply even to those who do not reference it, or perhaps even know which law applies.

Many of the cautionary statements give us a lesson in English grammar, by listing forward-looking words. Here is the shortest one I found, with only four, written by AbbVie:

> "The words 'believe,' 'expect,' 'anticipate,' 'project' and similar expressions and uses of future or conditional verbs, generally identify 'forward-looking statements ....'." [2]

(It seems they project or make projections, but not plans or forecasts!)

I found one that listed 23 forward-looking words, as if readers didn't know simple English and needed reminders. Two words ('believe' and 'expect') won the competition of the favourites, as they were included in every cautionary statement I read.

And then, there is the length of these forward-looking statements. Some are excruciatingly long. One has over 1,100 words. It's as though they're competing in a verbosity championship. Even the shortest, Abbott's, has 135 words. [3]

They all have a standard format giving us the following very interesting information (sarcasm of course):

1) The Form 10-K contains forward-looking statements from management based on forecasts, projections and another long list of similar words.
2) They give some forward-looking words as I show above.
3) They tell us the actual results may differ materially from the forecasts and projections in 1) above.
4) They say the said forecasts and projections may not be achieved.
5) Other unknown or future events may occur.
6) The company does not release revisions to the forward-looking statements in the Form 10-K if they turn out different.

Not only are they verbose, but they give us no new information.

I then checked to see how often Abbott's management change their forward-looking statements. I went back 20 years. The 135 words in their 2022 Form 10-K appeared in their 2002 Form 10-K except for two phrases: 'Item 1A. Risk Factors of this Form 10-K' and 'except as required by law'. In 2002, the statement went on for over 750 words, so someone took out a chunk of more than 600 words, but left the rest without changing the wording. Then, after 2008, they added: 'except as required by law' at the end, as a further precaution. So yes, management does review their statement, but only every 10 years or so.

Finally, my prize for the most elegant English in Cautionary Statements goes to a French company: Sanofi. They turned this dull subject into a little story. Here is an extract:

> "As a result of these factors, we cannot assure you that the forward-looking statements in this annual report will prove to be accurate. Furthermore, if our forward-looking statements prove to be inaccurate, the inaccuracy may be material. In light of the

significant uncertainties in these forward-looking statements, you should not regard these statements as a representation or warranty by us or any other person that we will achieve our objectives and plans in any specified time frame or at all."

It's almost a pleasure to read and, as a bonus, Sanofi cheekily repeat the word 'plan' in their list of forward-looking words, but don't feature them together. The first 'plan' comes in sixth place and the second comes in, symmetrically, twelfth, perhaps to please us as part of their literary endeavour, or perhaps as a gentle reminder in case we missed it the first time round! [4] Bravo to Sanofi.

[1] Several companies use this exact wording. Here are three of them: Novartis, Form 20-F for the fiscal year ended 31st December 2023; American Water Works Company Inc, Form 10-Q for the quarterly period ended 30th September 2019; The J.G. Wentworth Company, Form 10-K for the fiscal year ended 31st December 2017.

[2] AbbVie use this exact statement in many of their publications, in Form 10-K for the fiscal year ended 31st December 2022 and, for instance, in corporate announcements when relevant: https://news.abbvie.com/2024-02-22-AbbVie-and-Tentarix-Announce-Collaboration-to-Develop-Conditionally-Active,-Multi-Specific-Biologics-for-Oncology-and-Immunology. No need to invent a new one each time.

[3] Abbott Laboratories, Form 10-K, for the fiscal year ended 31st December 2022, page 15.

[4] Sanofi's forward-looking statement for 2022 can be found here: https://www.sanofi.com/assets/dotcom/content-app/documents/SAN_2022_20-F_Sanofi---accessible.pdf.

Predict the unpredictable

I wonder sometimes whether top management read their annual reports. If they did, they would realise that some of their assertions reach the level of silly and become entertaining. Here, for instance, are two typical statements taken from the risk factors section in the annual reports of the eight pharmaceutical companies.

"We are also unable to predict if and when any changes to laws or regulatory policies will occur and how they will affect our business …" [1]

"Abbott cannot predict the timing or impact of any future rulemaking or changes in the law." [2]

To put them into context, the first statement relates to the risk of delays in the development and commercialisation of new products. In the second the statement is part of Legal and Regulatory Risks.

Now what reasonable shareholder or simple reader of annual reports would expect management to predict future changes to any country's laws or regulatory policies? None. Note also that any information in annual reports only needs to be 'material' – insignificant risks need not be mentioned. Perhaps these two companies have information about changes in the law that will affect their business, but they cannot openly state what. I doubt it, but one never knows.

Johnson & Johnson tell us they are unable to predict the share price of their common stock. [3] Can anyone predict the trading price of any share in any company, or predict changes in foreign currency exchange rates? No, of course not. But Abbott insists they cannot predict changes in the exchange rates of their foreign currency. [4] I guess they believe they are the only company in the world that is unable to predict foreign currency exchange rates.

On the other hand, if top management have read these statements, and decided to keep them in their annual report, it tells us another story. I am sorry to say, I can only conclude that the companies consider both their reasonable shareholder and any simple reader to be either illiterate in business matters or complete idiots, or both.

[1] Bristol-Myers Squibb Company, Forms 10-K, for the fiscal years ended 31st December 2021, page 25 and 31st December 2022, page 24. The statement appears in both years with no change.

[2] Abbott Laboratories, Forms 10-K, for the fiscal years ended 31st December 2021, page 11 and 31st December 2022, page 11. The statement appears in both years with no change.

[3] Johnson & Johnson, annual report 2021, for the fiscal years ended 31st December 2021, page 14 and 31st December 2022, page 14. The statement appears in both years with no change.

[4] Abbott Laboratories, Forms 10-K, for the fiscal years ended 31st December 2021, page 13 and 31st December 2022, page 13. The statement appears in both years with no change.

An audit matters critically

Audit reports in the UK can be seven times longer than in the USA or the rest of Europe, sometimes even longer. Non-accountants might consider this logical; after all, auditors in the UK certify that financial statements are true and fair, whereas elsewhere they only need to certify that they are fair.

Similarly, auditors worry over their Critical Audit Matters more in the UK than elsewhere. Auditors in the two UK pharmaceutical companies (GSK and AstraZeneca), out of my eight, fretted over five or six Critical Audit Matters in each company, whereas the four USA pharmaceutical companies had a maximum of two.

Auditors use Critical Audit Matters to signify where they judge difficulty in auditing and to signal risks of material misstatement in the financial statements. Logically, therefore, UK companies are more difficult to audit and have more risk of misstatement, because they have more Critical Audit Matters. But could the issue lie with the auditors themselves rather than with the companies' location in the UK? The two auditors in these UK companies, PricewaterhouseCoopers and Deloitte, only signalled two Critical Audit Matters in their audits in the USA for Johnson & Johnson and Bristol Myers Squibb. So these two follow the trend of fewer audit matters in the USA.

Where the auditors agree is the critical matter of rebate accruals for US Medicaid and Medicare. Seven out of eight include the problem in their Critical Audit Matters even for UK companies. These rebates 'involve the use of significant assumptions and judgements in their calculations'. But 'given the complexity involved in determining these significant assumptions' [1] auditors worry about them. When they check assumptions and judgements that are significant and complex, they flip, because they in turn have to make their own assumptions and judgements about significance and complexity. So what is more natural than to tell everyone that their work is difficult?

The exception is Ernst & Young in their audit of Abbott. For them, rebate accruals are not an audit problem because management calculate them accurately. Abbott even congratulate themselves because their historic calculations of rebate accruals have always been close to actual. And the auditors, in their judgement, agree, because they have no Critical Audit Matters on this subject.

So we are left wondering why audit reports are so long in the UK. It's not to do with the difference between 'true and fair' and 'fairly stated'. Neither are British auditors more zealous or pernickety than their counterparts elsewhere. No. The real reason is UK auditors are excellent at following regulations, but why they put in so many Critical Audit Matters is a mystery we may never solve.

[1] These words come from Deloitte in their Critical Audit Matters of Bristol Myers Squibb. They explain the rebate problem the most clearly.

Exaggeration, boasting and complication

In reading the annual reports of grocery companies, I am struck by how differently they describe themselves. To muse a little, I make a comparison of six: three from the USA and three from the UK.

The most practical, down to earth, and simple is Target:

> "We are a general merchandise retailer selling products to our guests through our stores and digital channels."

Target choose to call their customers guests. None of the others go this far in hospitality.

Costco's description is also practical, but it's complicated, and they boast too much:

> "Costco Wholesale Corporation (Costco or the Company), a Washington corporation, and its subsidiaries operate membership warehouses based on the concept that offering members low prices on a limited selection of nationally branded and private-label products in a wide range of merchandise categories will produce high sales volumes and rapid inventory turnover."

Morrisons copy Costco's approach but boast even more: they have the right price, great choice, high quality and friendly colleagues. What more can one ask for? Here it is:

"The principal activities of Wm Morrison Supermarkets Limited and its subsidiaries are the retailing of food, clothing, general merchandise products and fuel throughout the United Kingdom.

Morrisons is a retailer, distributor, wholesaler and food manufacturer. We focus on ensuring that we offer the right price for our customers; have friendly colleagues in store; invest in our Market Street service counters; and provide a great choice of fresh, sustainably sourced, high quality produce, with strong links to local British growers and farmers."

Tesco are the champions of silliness (notwithstanding their claim to be champions for customers) with their emphasis on 'every day', and their exaggeration of 'serving the planet':

"The main activities of the Company and its subsidiaries are those of retailing and retail banking and insurance services.
Serving our customers, communities **and planet** a little better **every day**.

Tesco was built to be a champion for customers, serving them **every day** with affordable, healthy and sustainable food." (my bold text)

Associated British Foods are more modest, even in their boasting: safe, nutritious and affordable, but they are united in purpose:

"Associated British Foods is a highly diversified group, with a range of food and ingredients businesses as well as our retail brand, Primark. We are united in our purpose: to provide safe, nutritious and affordable food, and clothing that is great value for money."

Walmart wins the prize for all three: exaggeration, boasting and complication. Note how a simple exaggeration, like Tesco's 'every day', becomes a buzz with Walmart's 'anytime and anywhere'. They don't just have customer experience but customer-centric experience, and notice how they like these hyphenated adjectives. There are four of them. Finally, if you shop in Walmart, you live a better life and you don't spend money but save it. Here it is:

"Walmart Inc. is a people-led, technology-powered omni-channel [1] retailer dedicated to help people around the world save money and live better – anytime and anywhere – by providing the opportunity to shop in both retail stores and through eCommerce. Through innovation, the Company is striving to continuously improve a customer-centric experience that seamlessly integrates eCommerce and retail stores in an omni-channel offering that saves time for its customers."

[1] If you don't know what omni-channel means, and I didn't, it means a seamless customer experience. Omni-channel retailer sounds more technically sophisticated than the mere 'seamless customer experience retailer'. And within Walmart they are unsure (perhaps invisible internal controversy) – they sometimes write omni-channel as one unhyphenated word: omnichannel, but not in their annual reports.

FORMAL REPORTS
A number of approaches
I became suspicious in my first read of the report entitled 'IFRS 17 Insurance Contracts, Endorsement Criteria Assessment'. [1] On page 11, I found the term 'holistic approach'. *"What is a holistic approach?"* I asked myself, reaching for my *Oxford English Dictionary*. Holism has no relevance to international accounting standards, as far as I can tell. It is used in medicine, psychology and philosophy, not accounting. And then I read the whole sentence, and my suspicions were confirmed. I had to read the sentence three times to even partially understand it. Here it is:

> "1.8 A holistic approach has been taken to the assessment of whether a standard is not contrary to the principle that both the individual and consolidated financial statements must give a true and fair view ..."

I understand at last that the United Kingdom Endorsement Board (UKEB) want to assess IFRS 17 as a whole and not just as the sum of its parts in relation to a true and fair view. Even today, I don't know how they did it, nor did I discover what their holistic approach really is.

This made me wonder how many different 'approaches' the board would take to assess IFRS 17. I struck gold two pages later when I found their second approach: an exceptions-based approach. I am not sure what an exceptions-based approach is either, but it no longer matters.

I had to see how many approaches the UK Endorsement Board could invent. Believe it or not, there are 21 in this report! They are all over the place. I list them in alphabetical order:

> Annuity profit recognition approaches
> Bottom-up approach
> CSM allocation approach (or an appropriate approach to allocating CSM)
> Disaggregation approaches
> Exceptions-based approach
> Fair value approach (FVA)
> Fully retrospective approach
> Fully retrospective transition approach
> Holistic approach
> Modified retrospective approach
> More prescriptive approach
> Peers' approaches
> Premium allocation approach
> Principles-based approach
> Realistic balance sheet approach
> Revenue recognition approach
> The Green Book approach
> The standard's approach
> Top-down approach
> Variable Fee Approach (VFA)
> Wider transformation approaches

As you can see, some of the approaches are listed as plural, so the actual number of them is presumably much higher than 21.

My favourite is The Green Book approach, [2] well known in HM Treasury circles, unknown in accounting circles, but clearly precious for assessing international accounting standards, given it has absolutely no relation to accounting, accountants or finance. It gives civil servants guidance on evaluating government policies among other things. Not to be confused with the 'Green Book' (as the UK government's publication *Immunisation against infectious disease* is commonly known) or the 2018 film *Green Book* directed by Peter Farrelly.

Do not mix up the VFA with the FVA or you might become confused. The two approaches are not related but, because they use the same initials in a different order, one has to be careful when identifying them. Everyone knows top-down and bottom-up approaches, but who can guess what a fully retrospective transition approach could mean.

If you don't know what the initials CSM stand for, they represent Contractual Service Margin, but when this is added to an allocation approach, it becomes unnecessarily complicated. And if you don't know what this phrase means, it is a much-used term for experts working in profit recognition in annuities.

The Peers' approaches surprised me. I wasn't sure who the peers are, the FASB perhaps, or a group of Lords who happen to have an approach relevant to IFRS 17; probably both, because there are more than one. The prescriptive approach means nothing to me, nor does the 'more prescriptive' one relevant here.

And, finally, there were many generic references to the different approaches the board had to take on their long approach, all 11 of them. They had, for instance, a few 'new approaches'. Here are another nine: consistent, practical, appropriate, retrospective, detailed, single, correct, applicable and different. Do not forget the last, a double adjective plural of 'different practical approaches'.

I had approached reading this report with dread, thinking I would pass a tedious hour. But, no, what fun I had: the thorough exploration of the central imagery of approaching, the satisfaction of reaching the last approach on page 182, then the disappointing ending, with no approach on the last page, perhaps setting up an approach for the sequel. I look forward to it in their review of IFRS 18, where I anticipate they will beat their record of 220 appearances of the word 'approach'.

[1] IFRS 17 Insurance Contracts, Endorsement Criteria Assessment issued by the United Kingdom Endorsement Board, May 2022.

[2] The Green Book is guidance issued by HM Treasury on how to appraise policies, programmes and projects: https://www.gov.uk/government/publications/the-green-book-appraisal-and-evaluation-in-central-government/the-green-book-2020.

Sinking feeling

I was reading quietly through the IAASB's *Handbook of International Quality Control, Auditing, Review, Other Assurance, and Related Services Pronouncements* for the first time (the title is a mouthful) and skipping through the Glossary of Terms, which, would you believe, runs to 18 pages. I had not even reached the Contents section, when I had my first surprise. I discovered the word 'sink'.

What a relief I felt when I saw it had no relation to the kitchen type. And then another surprise: sink is a physical unit or process. What sort of accounting process could be a 'sink'? I wondered.

Here it is:

> "Sink – A physical unit or process that removes GHGs from the atmosphere." [1]

It must be that I didn't know what GHG meant. So I investigated further. Of course GHG stands for greenhouse gases and the same accounting manual gave me their definition, on page 17:

> "Greenhouse gases (GHGs)—Carbon dioxide (CO2) and any other gases required by the applicable criteria to be included in the GHG statement, such as: methane; nitrous oxide; sulfur hexafluoride; hydrofluorocarbons; perfluorocarbons; and chlorofluorocarbons. Gases other than carbon dioxide are often expressed in terms of carbon dioxide equivalents (CO2-e)."

But this didn't help either. I wondered why these two definitions were part of the glossary of terms of an auditing manual. And then I discovered many more related definitions, such as emissions, emission deductions, emissions factor, and GHG statement.

But my surprise turned into astonishment when I discovered that these definitions, though included in the Glossary of Terms, did not appear anywhere in the body of Volume 1 of the 2021 edition of the

Handbook of International Quality Control, Auditing, Review, Other Assurance, and Related Services Pronouncements, all 900 pages.

What, I thought, is the point of defining 'sink' and other GHG terms when they write nothing about them? Either the IAASB are collectively going mad or this must be a mistake. But I guess neither, as they follow the now fairly common custom of a glossary that defines random words that don't appear in the publication!

But I continued my search anyway. What about Volume 2? I thought. Here, I discovered the 'International Standard on Assurance Engagements (ISAE) 3410', where the auditor is required to ensure that the GHG statement is free from material misstatement.

The IAASB gave me a fright. But they are not mad; auditors are required to investigate 'sink'. What a relief.

[1] International Auditing and Assurance Standards Board, IAASB, *Handbook of International Quality Control, Auditing, Review, Other Assurance, and Related Services Pronouncements*, 2021 Edition Volume 1, Glossary of Terms, page 26.

Licence agreement of the FASB

From the beginning, I sensed I could have some fun with the License Agreement of the FASB Accounting Standards Codification. To access their standards, they forced me to accept the agreement with a 'click' of my Bluetooth mouse on the 'I agree' button, before being allowed to read it.

This was my clue, and I wasn't disappointed. The agreement is a classic of too many lawyers given too much power, or 'over lawyering' as they say in the USA, so I have to tell you about it.

It starts with an order in capitals to CAREFULLY READ LICENSE AGREEMENT, which is what I did. I found the document terrifying and amusing at the same time. And the number of things they asked me to do was amazing.

Among the many, here are the ones that most concerned me:

1) First come two warnings, not only in capitals but also in bold capital letters, where they tell me I can only use the Codification for my personal use and not commercially.

> They do not specify what they mean by personal use, and surely, I thought, if I write a book and sell it, then this is commercial. Therefore, I cannot use anything from the Codification.
>
> 2) The agreement then goes on to tell me that I cannot copy anything from the Codification or commercially exploit it. Now I have no idea how to commercially exploit anything, but I do need to copy parts of the Codification, if only to quote the relevant parts for my book. But I am not allowed to copy quotes onto my computer.

If I have to ask the FASB's permission to use material in the Codification, I have to copy the said material into my computer before asking their permission. How can I ask permission for a quote without copying it into my computer to tell them I need permission for it. Quite illogical.

> 3) Then came something which surprised me. They do not allow me to use the initials FASB, not only without permission but also without their prior consent **in writing**.

I must have used FASB more than a hundred times in this book without their prior consent. What are they going to do about this?

They then go on to ask me to do something that I refuse point blank to do. It is not a request, but a given, because remember I clicked on the 'I accept' button agreeing to ALL the conditions of the agreement.

> 4) I have to agree to tell the FAF immediately (note the 'immediately' but with no definition; after an hour, a day, a week?) if anyone uses the Codification through me.

I must denounce somebody, betray them to the FAF, and this is written in the agreement! And who is the FAF anyway? (Well, I and all accountants in the USA will know perfectly well that it's the Financial Accounting Foundation. Others may not.) You will remember that the FAF is the organisation that controls the FASB, the Financial Accounting Standards Board.

Plus, I must indemnify the FAF for any losses they might incur as a result of the actions of this hypothetical person.

Well, what is obvious is that the Foundation wants my money, not the FASB. Why am I even surprised at that?

At this point, I was halfway down page 2 of the five-page agreement. What else could they possibly want from me? But then, as a distraction, I noticed that the words You and Your in the agreement are written with a capital Y, referencing me. That made me feel important.

I then moved on to page 3, and I came across a remarkable sentence. I paraphrase:

6) I agree that everything I read in the Agreement is reasonable.

I stopped reading and waited for a full minute in complete astonishment. But I do not agree that the Agreement is reasonable. How can I possibly agree, given my complaints listed above? What's more, I hadn't finished reading it yet. But I had already agreed, because I had clicked on the 'I accept' button! So I read on, agreeing but not wanting to agree.

The second half of page 3 is again in bold capitals. This, I guess, is standard Blah Blah on disclaimers and limited liability.

7) I am informed in bold capitals that if I use the Codification, I do so at my personal risk.

'Sole risk' and 'sole personal use' – I was now feeling quite alone.

8) And then I read that I agree to pay the FAF millions of dollars 'in the event of' ... followed by a long list of actions I must never make, or else. I decided not to read them. I found it too tedious.

But not before seeing a vital sentence that I did actually agree with:

9) Whereby if there are any mistakes in the Codification I accept them.

Excellent, this is what my book is all about – looking for 'faults' and writing about them. So perhaps they won't attack me after all.

But again, I am in a bind. If I find the faults in the Codification and take the micky out of the FASB when I write about them, what will they do? I cannot see them giving me permission to highlight their faults and laugh at their exaggerations.

10) Finally, the FAF tells me that they can modify the Agreement without telling me and naturally I agree with whatever modification they come up with in advance, regardless of what they write. That is no longer a surprise.

I saw with profound relief that page 5 consisted of only two lines. But, by this time, these 10 requests had exhausted me, even if all I had done was to click on the 'I agree' button.

Some might think this is standard American legalese, but some of the things they ask me to do are so complicated, so outrageous, that they amuse me. I then discovered the agreement doesn't apply to me. I had wasted my time reading it and writing about it, and the FAF had wasted their time writing it and publishing it. It doesn't apply to me because of the concept of 'fair use'. In its simplest form 'fair use' means that if I reproduce a small amount of the FASB Accounting Standards Codification, I can ignore the agreement. But it entertained me so much, I had to write about it.

P.S. I wanted to copy the License Agreement of the FASB Accounting Standards Codification in its entirety, all 3,200 words, as an annex to this book, just in case they realise their excess, and either simplify it or take it out. However, the FAF refused permission, or, in their own words: "We would not grant a right to reprint it (the License Agreement) in its entirety given the nature of the materials." So you will have to look it up yourself 'given the nature of the materials'! You will find the agreement at https://asc.fasb.org/Login, by first clicking on the affirmation that you are not a robot, and then clicking on 'Access'.

P.P.S. I sent the FASB agreement to a lawyer friend for review. At first, he didn't see the ludicrous or amusing. He went right into the legal technicalities, and it took a couple of email exchanges for him to see the exaggeration and the fun to be had with it.

P.P.P.S. Given my dismay at the FASB, I checked with the IASB. Despite having headquarters in London, the IFRS Foundation is incorporated in Delaware so is also a US Foundation. I checked their site to see what agreement they would force on me when I read their IASB standards. Their terms and conditions are nearly twice the length of the FAF's, at some 6,000 words, so it seems their lawyers also had a field day preparing them. However, they do not require the unreasonable. One major difference, though, is that the IFRS Foundation require me to pay a subscription to read their standards in their entirety, whereas the FAF no longer requests this, because their Codification is free, except for the promise to sell my soul and more to them.

Chapter 2

Silly Fun

JARGON
Accountants are concerned about going
To apply the going concern concept, accountants have to ask themselves whether a company has the 'capacity to continue in operation' in the future (to use the term employed by the *Oxford English Dictionary*). Or, more simply, is the company going bankrupt? If the answer is no, the company is a going concern, and all is well. The difficulty arises when accountants don't know or can't tell because of the poor financial situation of the company. Regardless, they have to decide.

Accountants within the company are always biased towards maintaining their business as a going concern, but their job is to get the auditors to agree. This can be a grey area, and is often complicated for all concerned. But accountants make it more complicated by defining going concern in different ways. The FASB in the USA have one definition. The IASB, which covers most of the rest of the world, have another, and both have chosen not to define going concern in the positive, but to define when a company is not a going concern. This, they believe, makes it easier.

Both boards agree it is a question of judgement and both agree that it relates to 'doubt'. But not the same doubt. In IFRS it is 'significant doubt'. Under US GAAP it is 'substantial doubt'.

> "Substantial doubt about the company's ability to continue as a going concern." (FASB)
>
> "Significant doubt upon the company's ability to continue as a going concern." (IASB)

Now what on earth is the difference between significant and substantial? And does it matter in this context? It must matter to the two accounting bodies, otherwise they would have agreed to use the same word. The FASB, for instance, could have used significant doubt because, in the Master Glossary of their Accounting Standards Codification, they use the word 'significant' for their term 'significant influence'. But they choose 'substantial' for going concern.

I believe that 'substantial' is stronger than 'significant', and the *Oxford English Dictionary* seems to agree with me, albeit in a rather hesitant sort of way. One of its definitions of 'substantial' states 'of real significance'. [1] So, not run-of-the-mill significance, but real significance. I am not sure what 'of unreal significance' would look like. On the other hand, in one of its definitions of 'significant', it uses the word 'substantial', [1] so perhaps they are interchangeable after all. But still, to me, 'doubt of real significance' remains stronger than 'significant doubt'.

In an attempt to help us overcome this confusion, the FASB give more information on what they mean by 'substantial'. Substantial doubt exists when 'it is probable that the entity will be unable to meet its obligations ...' [2] This suggests that the FASB believe substantial to mean probable. But they don't stop there – they tell us what probable means too:

> "Probable: The future event or events are likely to occur." [2]

Substantial means probable means likely to occur. This doesn't help – it confuses us even more. The FASB's definition could therefore be:

> "The future event: The company's inability to continue as a going concern is likely to occur."

But this doesn't sound quite the same as their definition of significant doubt.

The IASB, on the other hand, don't explain their 'significant'. They leave us to pick up the *Oxford English Dictionary* as I did.

I then checked on what the auditors in the IAASB think. In their handbook, they do not recognise substantial doubt in relation to going concern, only significant doubt. I guess they consider these two phrases mean the same thing, without telling us.

To conclude, the two accounting bodies use the same word, doubt about going concern, but give it different definitions to come to the same meaning. Mischievous, no doubt on purpose.

[1] *Oxford English Dictionary*, Substantial: 4. Firmly or solidly established; of solid worth or value; of real significance, weighty; reliable; important, worthwhile. Significant: 4b. In weakened sense: noticeable, substantial, considerable, large.

[2] Financial Accounting Standards Board, Accounting Standards Codification, ASC, 205, Presentation of Financial Statements, 40 Going Concern.

Lying under

Would you believe me if I found the accounting term 'underlying' 280 times in an annual report? Unilever are the culprit. They use the word so often I found it comical after a few pages.

This is my favourite underlying statement. It even has a value of €6,568 million:

> "Underlying profit attributable to shareholders' equity – used for underlying earnings per share."

What, I wonder, is 'the profit attributable to shareholders' equity – used for earnings per share' without the qualifying 'underlyings', calculated by nearly every other company? I searched for it without success.

When I reached their note on taxation, I was relieved to find a table reconciling the computed rate of tax to the underlying effective tax rate to the effective tax rate. But my relief didn't last long. I discovered, with dismay, that the computed rate of tax is a calculation, weighted by the amount of underlying profit before taxation. I can only conclude that this computed rate of tax is actually an 'underlying computed tax rate'.

Unilever highlight other non-accounting underlying items, making them even more comical, for instance underlying reward principles and underlying causes. And, finally, they have transferred their underlying habit to the auditors, who write in their report about 'underlying documentation' and 'underlying exposure' instead of mere documentation and exposure.

But Unilever go even further. They invent 'non-underlying':

"Profit on this disposal was €2,303 million, recognised as a non-underlying item."

I wonder what a non-underlying item is. I presume it has been taken out of their underlying calculations.

I then checked two other British annual reports, by bp and Legal & General, to see what they think. bp are not as prolific as Unilever but they still use the term 'underlying' 160 times. Legal & General clock up a more modest 50.

I then checked some US annual reports to see if underlying is uniquely British. It is and it isn't. Bristol Myers Squibb use the term underlying about 115 times, but never in an accounting context. They include phrases such as 'underlying business performance' or 'underlying economic exposure' but never as part of the financial statements. Johnson & Johnson follow the usage of Bristol Myers Squibb but with fewer underlying terms, less than 20.

Having read so few annual reports, I cannot reach a firm conclusion on whether companies use underlying often or not. But I do conclude that Unilever's is comical. I recommend you read their 2022 annual report yourself, if only the first couple of pages. Their excessive number of 'underlyings' makes their report sound silly to me.

Unwinding the uplift

Uplift is one of the words chosen as jargon by accountants, but not always with the same meaning. Which of the meanings do they use? The Scottish give uplift three different meanings according to the *Oxford English Dictionary*. [1] Could the accountants have taken the origin from them?

The first Scottish meaning makes someone proud. Accountants are not interested in pride, so they don't use it in this way. The second is in the collecting of rent or wages. Now, this is closer to the accounting world but, again, accountants choose not to use it in this sense. Nor do accountants use uplift in the sense of what lingerie can do. The closest accountants get to one of the meanings of uplift is the Scottish sense of picking up passengers in a bus – the movement upwards of climbing onto the bus.

But accountants use uplift not in the sense of 'climbing' but 'increase'. The expression, for instance, 'the Group (and doesn't matter which group) has elected not to uplift the book value' means the Group has elected not to increase the book value. Or 'an uplift of $5,630m on the carrying value' means an increase of $5,630m on the carrying value. How much easier it would have been to use the word 'increase' in these sentences.

Many accountants use uplift with another accounting term 'fair value', as in fair value uplift. But then they decide to decrease what they have just increased and this expression becomes 'fair value uplift unwind'. Accountants don't do themselves any favours when they use a statement like this. Initially, I decided not to name the company that put this into their annual report to avoid embarrassing them. Later, I changed my mind. AstraZeneca are the culprits.

But they are not alone. GSK, for instance, write that 'fair value uplift is expected to unwind', which is a little easier to understand. An easier version is 'release of fair value uplift'.

Some companies don't use unwind with uplift – the BBB, for instance. In their 2022 annual report they only used unwind once: a 'deferred tax balances unwind', whereas in 2023 unwinding appears five times. Instead of 'decrease', they include comments such as the value of 'investments were likely to unwind this year' or 'this unwinding of previous unrealised gains may well continue over the next 12–18 months'. Unwinding has become popular for the BBB in 2023, but no longer for deferred taxes.

And then, from time to time, accountants change the meaning of uplift from 'increase' to something else. Here's GSK again:

> "We have commenced biodiversity uplift projects at our three largest R&D facilities." [2]

I have no idea what this means. Believe me, even putting it in context does not make it clearer.

And then there is this, which I suppose uses uplift as a sort of moral elevation:

> "When we talk about uplifting our associates, it certainly includes compensation." [3]

Or perhaps they are using the Scottish meaning of making their employees proud to work for their company, even though they are based in Cincinnati, Ohio.

[1] *Oxford English Dictionary*, Uplift 1.c. 1863–Scottish. To make proud. 3.a. 1508–Scottish. To collect, levy (rents, etc.); to draw (wages). 3.b. 1961– More generally, to collect or pick up (something other than money); spec. of a bus: to take up (passengers). Chiefly Scottish.

[2] GSK Inc, Form 20-F, for the fiscal year ended 31st December 2022, page 46.

[3] The Kroger Co., for the fiscal year ended 29th January 2022, Notice of 2022 Annual Meeting of Shareholders 2022 Proxy Statement and 2021 Annual Report on Form 10-K, Dear Fellow Shareholder letter, under the heading Investing in Our Associates, second paragraph.

Ride over management

I guess non-accountants, and even some accountants, have no idea what management override means. It has nothing to do with management riding camels in the desert on a team-building exercise. Nor is it connected to overdrive when racing these same camels. I recently discovered the term in the audit report of Associated British Foods. The auditors, Ernst & Young, consider that there could be 'pressure on management to manipulate revenue recognition'.

And they go on:

> "There is a risk that management may override controls intentionally to misstate revenue transactions."

Management may misstate and even manipulate revenues on purpose without detection. Wow! And then the auditors did something that surprised me. They decided not to test the internal controls around revenue recognition:

> "We did not test the operating effectiveness of these controls."

I thought auditors always checked internal control.

However, and I guess this is the important part, they then list the audit work they performed to make sure that management didn't manipulate revenues. They, for instance, obtained third-party confirmations and performed 'hindsight analysis', whatever this might be. An interesting if unusual audit test, and one I have never heard of.

I checked on the ICAEW site to see if override existed. I am, perhaps, the ignorant one. I was relieved when the message came up: 'Sorry, no results found.' But the site suggested I check my spelling and asked if I wanted to find a chartered accountant to help me out. I did check my spelling but did not take up their offer to look for a chartered accountant.

To continue, Ernst & Young made these audit tests, including, no doubt, multiple hindsight analyses, in 82 locations covering '85% of the Group's revenue' and satisfied themselves that management wasn't dishonest. They concluded:

> "We did not identify any evidence of management override or material misstatement in the revenue recognised."

Having satisfied themselves that all was well, why, I wonder, did the auditors bring up the problem in the first place, and make such a scathing Key Audit Matter? A problem that no longer exists. We will never know. Auditors' judgement, I suppose.

Clean or dirty

An accounting 'clean' does not have an opposite in 'dirty'. Accountants make it more complicated than that. They don't use 'clean' as a noun, as in 'give it a clean', nor as a verb as 'in clean your shoes', nor as an adverb as in the well-known cricketing expression 'clean bowled'. They use it as an official adjective to describe an opinion:

"The auditor has concluded an unmodified (i.e., 'clean') opinion is appropriate based on the audit evidence obtained." [1]

Clean means 'unmodified' to auditors. I find it amazing that the IAASB need to explain what unmodified means by using jargon – clean – and not vice versa. But even an unmodified or clean opinion means nothing to the ordinary person. It just means the financial statements are okay. The balance sheet is clean. All is well.

Even more amazingly, the opposite of clean is not 'modified' but 'qualified'. I am a qualified accountant, which is considered positive. But a qualified audit opinion is negative. It means that the financial statements do not present fairly the financial results. A modified audit report means nothing to accountants, nor does a dirty opinion.

So the opposite of clean is qualified, not dirty. Beware!

[1] International Auditing and Assurance Standards Board, IAASB, *Handbook of International Quality Control, Auditing, Review, Other Assurance, and Related Services Pronouncements*, 2021 Edition Volume 1, page 416.

STANDARDS
Material definitions differ

The two accounting boards use the word 'material' in the same way but, and this is ludicrous, they have different definitions.

Material for an accountant has nothing to do with building materials or dressmaking and no connection to cloth or clothes. Accountants use the word in the sense of significant or important. And they use it specifically in the preparation and audit of financial statements as a sort of liability insurance. Accountants prepare financial statements and ensure they include no important errors. If someone finds an unimportant error, it doesn't count.

The two boards agree in three ways. They both define materiality in the negative, both in relation to financial statements, and both use the theoretical user of financial statements as the decision maker, to decide whether something is 'material' or not. But this is all.

The FASB are emphatic in their definition of where a 'reasonable person would change his or her judgement'. The IASB are not so sure. As you already know, their 'primary user could reasonably be expected to make a different decision'. The IASB have obscuring in the definition, the FASB do not.

Here is a summary of the main differences:

FASB	IASB
reasonable person	primary user
would	could reasonably be expected
judgement	decision
	obscuring

The two definitions are different, but is a material value under FASB standards different from a material value under IASB standards, under the same circumstances?

The FASB have been jumping around with their definitions of material. They changed it in 1980, and again in 2010. In August 2018, the FASB changed its definition of 'materiality', reverting back to its original definition from 1980. What a lot of time and intellectual accounting thinking must have gone into deciding that!

Then, perhaps in retaliation, the IASB also changed theirs in 2020, as I explained in Chapter 1. This change moves the definitions further apart.

Primary or reasonable
The IASB become specific with their 'primary users' of financial statements. Only these users are concerned with materiality. The FASB disagree, saying that materiality is wider; it concerns any 'reasonable person', who makes a judgement on these same financial statements. A primary user is not the same as a reasonable person. Remember, we are back on the Clapham omnibus.

Would or could
The FASB are assertive when applying materiality. They use the word 'would', as in 'would be influenced' by a misstatement. The IFRS are more careful, using 'could reasonably be expected' to be influenced by a misstatement. 'Would' is clear and to the point. It has a certainty to it. 'Could reasonably be expected to' is more willy-nilly, vague and uncertain. There is an element of dancing around the bush, but given

the uncertainty, perhaps tiptoeing around the issue reflects the process better.

The IFRS could have stepped in when they modified their definition by putting in 'would' to be aligned with the FASB definition, but they didn't. They knew what the FASB had done in 2018 and why. They considered using 'would' and rejected it:

> "The Board concluded that using 'would' would be a substantive change that might have unintended consequences."

How terrible could the consequences of using 'would' possibly be? They don't tell us. Instead, the IFRS took out their simple 'could' and watered it down to their 'could reasonably be expected to', pushing it even further apart from the FASB's 'would'.

To be fair though, the FASB had their hands tied when choosing 'would'. The Supreme Court, in a case in 1976, used 'would' and not 'could' (and certainly not 'could reasonably be expected') when deciding on what is 'material', so they had no choice. The Court stated:

> "An omitted fact is material if there is a substantial likelihood that a reasonable shareholder *would* consider it important in deciding how to vote."

We are back to the word 'reasonable' again. The Clapham omnibus made it all the way to Australia but bypassed the USA. A pity!

Obscuring

The IASB added 'obscuring' to their definition in 2020. For them, it is important even if they don't explain clearly what it is. Obscuring information to a non-accountant is hiding information. The FASB have decided not to specify 'obscuring' or anything similar. Hiding something material, in a mountain of immaterial information, is not part of the definition of material for FASB, although they sort of imply it with the phrase 'the magnitude of the item is such that it is probable', where omission can be associated with hiding or obscuring.

What does this tell us?
So what does this tell us about the two bodies? Mainly, that they complicate their lives with intellectual details that seem important to them. Either the two definitions give the same material value, or the FASB definition gives a different value of material to the IASB's. Both leave me speechless for their silliness, but perhaps I am the only one who notices or cares.

Work together to make a frame

When is a framework a standard? In 2010, the IASB issued an 86-page document called 'Conceptual Framework for Financial Reporting', [1] which describes the objectives and concepts for general purpose financial reporting. And in the second paragraph complication begins:

> "The Conceptual Framework is not a Standard. Nothing in the Conceptual Framework overrides any Standard or any requirement in a Standard."

Or, put another way, Standards always overrule the Framework. So some IFRS Standards do comply with the Conceptual Framework. BUT it doesn't state which Standards differ, where they differ or how they differ. So to understand the framework, one needs to read ALL the standards, and refer back to the framework. How complicated is that?

Which parts of the framework are obsolete? Are there many differences? Are they so few that it doesn't matter? Are they important differences or minor ones? The IASB remains silent on these questions.

The opposite is also true. Some Standards refer to the Conceptual Framework to confirm it, and they become part of the Standards. This happens in the very first International Accounting Standard, IAS1, [2] where the definition of assets, liabilities, income and expenses in the Conceptual Framework become part of the standard.

But when one reads these definitions in the Conceptual Framework, one cannot tell if they have been overridden or confirmed by a later standard or not.

Is this an oversight or a deliberate attempt by the IASB to make consultation of the Conceptual Framework complicated? Let's go back to the first sentence to see the objectives. Perhaps this will answer my question:

> "The Conceptual Framework for Financial Reporting (Conceptual Framework) describes the objective of, and the concepts for, general purpose financial reporting."

The objective of financial reporting is clear and requires no comment from me: to provide useful financial information about the reporting entity. But the IASB get themselves in a muddle by mentioning concepts. There are only three rather obscure ones in the framework: concepts of capital, concepts of capital maintenance and measurement concepts. That's all! Are there others so obvious that they don't need to state them as concepts? Or must the reader guess them? Perhaps the reader knows them. I don't but it doesn't matter.

In section 1.11 the IASB do give us a clue how to identify the concepts they have not named. They state that financial reports are based mostly on estimates, judgements and models, and they then add:

> "The Conceptual Framework establishes the concepts that underlie those estimates, judgements and models."

So each time an estimate, a judgement or a model is mentioned, the reader must look for the concept behind it. In theory this is clear, but then, in the sentence after, they mess it up completely by stating:

> "The concepts are the goal towards which the Board and preparers of financial reports strive."

Concepts have become 'the goal'. That does not make sense to me. I suppose they mean that the combined concepts make up the overall goal for the preparation of financial reports, but to state 'concepts are a goal' is silly.

So there you are. The concepts are not identified; the reader has to search them out and combine them together to discover the goal of preparing financial reports under IASB standards.

[1] Conceptual Framework for Financial Reporting, issued by the International Accounting Standards Board in September 2010 and revised in March 2018.

[2] International Accounting Standard 1, Presentation of Financial Statements, Paragraph 15. Conceptual Framework for Financial Reporting.

If, and only if

By the time I got to the third 'if, and only if' in IAS 36, I started to worry. Then, I realised the writer must be a frustrated mathematician, pining after times spent on Boolean algebra, where 'A *if and only if* B' means that A is true if B is true, and B is true if A is true, sometimes written as iff. I read on hoping for another 'if, and only if' represented by iff. I found two more, but no iff. I searched hopelessly for the sixth, certain that my frustrated mathematician would slip in a discreet iff.

Let's take one of the 'if, and only if's'. I couldn't find one more important than another, so I chose the shortest:

> "If, and only if, the recoverable amount of an asset is less than its carrying amount, the carrying amount of the asset shall be reduced to its recoverable amount." [1]

This sentence sounds silly from multiple repetitions of 'if', 'asset', 'carrying', 'recoverable' and 'amount', so the insistent 'if, and only if' becomes ridiculous. But mathematicians then repeat numbers indefinitely.

And then I discovered that the mathematician's cousin must have written IAS 40 and IAS 41, borrowing the same technique, but using a different phrase, not to be accused of being a copycat. Here, the choice is 'when, and only when'.

I chose an easy one to understand:

> "An entity shall transfer a property to, or from, investment property when, and only when, there is a change in use." [2]

Now transferring property in and out of investment is such a frequent and, above all, important accounting occurrence, this 'when' phrase becomes a must. Note the sarcasm!

Sometimes, the two scatter their standards with the less emphatic 'only if' and 'only when'. The two must have written IAS 37 together, as evidenced by their choice of all four expressions: 'if, and only if', 'only if', 'when and only when' and 'only when'. Eight times! It is easy to identify the standards not written by these two mathematicians. They never have these phrases.

The IASB sprinkle some of their standards with the threatening phrases of 'if, and only if' and 'when, and only when'. The threat, though, is a hollow one. What happens to an accountant who doesn't follow their emphatic instruction? They never explain, because there are no consequences.

[1] International Accounting Standard 36 Impairment of Assets, IAS 36, paragraph 59.
[2] International Accounting Standard 40 Investment Property, IAS 40, paragraph 57.

Accounting uncertainty

Accountants adore uncertainty so much that they invent and define several different versions of it. I found the first one in the Conceptual Framework for Financial Reporting issued by the IASB, called measurement uncertainty. But there are others.

Measurement uncertainty arises when (to use their pompous words) a monetary amount needs to be estimated. That is simple, but it covers many accounting events in the financial statements. I find it interesting that auditors decided not to use this term. The International Auditing and Assurance Standards Board acknowledge this in their *Handbook*:

> "Susceptibility to a lack of precision in measurement is often referred to in accounting frameworks as measurement uncertainty." [1]

But they dismiss the term out of hand with no explanation and replace it with **their** term: 'estimation uncertainty'. Let me show you their two definitions to enable you to measure the significance of their choices:

Measurement uncertainty	Susceptibility to a lack of precision in measurement
Estimation uncertainty	Susceptibility to an inherent lack of precision in measurement [1]

One extra word: 'inherent' is so much more precise than 'lack' on its own! They must consider 'inherent' to be critical, but despite four more paragraphs of explanation I cannot understand why. The IAASB do try to help by explaining their meaning of inherent. Here it is:

"The lack of precision in measurement arising from these constraints is inherent because it cannot be eliminated from the measurement process."

So we have constraints and a measurement process, but to add to the complication, they add outcomes or, more precisely, 'directly observable outcomes' and 'measurement basis' – not to be confused with measurement uncertainty. Clear as mud.

But wait, there's more! The Board have added two levels of estimation uncertainty: significant estimation uncertainty and high estimation uncertainty. I won't bore you by explaining the difference between the two, nor which is worse, significant or high!

But I deviate from my initial explanation. Measurement uncertainty and estimation uncertainty are the first two official versions. The third is existence uncertainty. Or to make it simple:

"In some cases, it is uncertain whether an obligation exists." [2]

Or whether an asset or liability, or even any accounting vehicle, exists.

The fourth official version is outcome uncertainty, which discusses economic benefits that may or may not flow through the accounting systems.

So we have four uncertainties and two sub-uncertainties:

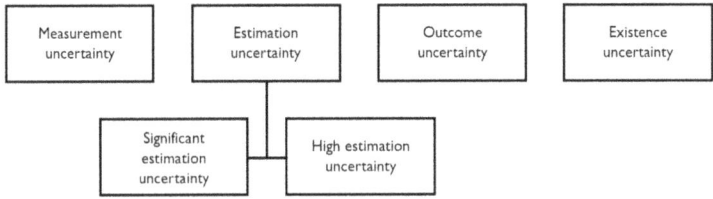

Finally, this beautiful 'Beware' statement tells us not to become confused about the different uncertainties:

> "Measurement uncertainty is different from both outcome uncertainty and existence uncertainty ..."

So there you are. They are different. (It really exists: have a look on page A76.) [3]

I then checked to see how the auditors (the IAASB) audit outcome uncertainty and existence uncertainty. They don't. They ignore them completely. They put no reference to them in their handbook. In place of outcome uncertainty, they think the phrase 'outcome of the measurement or evaluation' is better. For existence uncertainty, they use expressions such as 'existence and completeness of transactions' as a substitute.

I guess by changing and ignoring these expressions, the IAASB are discreetly snubbing the IASB. But I cannot imagine why.

[1] International Auditing and Assurance Standards Board, IAASB, *Handbook of International Quality Control, Auditing, Review, Other Assurance, and Related Services Pronouncements*, 2021 Edition Volume 1, page 377.

[2] International Accounting Standards Board, IAS, Conceptual Framework for Financial Reporting, September 2010, revised March 2018, Paragraph 4.35, page A44.

[3] International Accounting Standards Board, IAS, Conceptual Framework for Financial Reporting, September 2010, revised March 2018, Paragraph 6.61, page A76.

The imaginary Chief Operating Decision Maker

IFRS 8 introduces the Chief Operating Decision Maker, a fictitious position that accountants must search for in order to apply the standard. This elusive decision maker can be found by detecting managers who review operating results, regardless of their official title. But not all operating results – only those with a threshold greater than 10% of revenues, profits or assets. Any one of the three will do.

As a definition, this inverted four-step process must be one of the most complicated ever. Imagine inventing a fictitious manager, searching for them in the company by looking at only those who review operating results, calculating 10%, and – success! – you have found a segment. If you cannot find the manager or the operating results, no segment reporting is necessary.

I guess, by now, there is a chance that you won't believe me, so I have put the full definition of an operating segment below. [1]

The writers of the standard are well aware of the complexity of the subject and have given us a practical clue to help us navigate through it. They declare in paragraph 7 that a Chief Operating Decision Maker is 'not necessarily a manager with a specific title'. Not much help. But they do give a practical clue. Our fictitious manager could actually be called the Chief Operating Officer. At last, something concrete to work with.

Would you believe there is another Chief Operating Decision Maker in the FASB Accounting Standards Codification? But he or she does not have quite the same function as the one defined by the IASB. The Codification defines the person more specifically as either the chief executive officer or the chief operating officer, but not always, only often. [2] So now they have two possible positions in the company.

But these two managers do not define the segments in the FASB standards; they are decided by an undefined concept called the 'management approach', [2] which is based on the organisation of the company and way decisions are made.

But both boards complicate the situation further by inventing yet another hypothetical manager: the fictional segment manager who reports directly to the fictional Chief Operating Decision Maker. [3] By summarising the segment manager's tasks in a mini job description, they claim this helps us define an Operating Segment under IFRS, whereas under the Codification the hypothetical segment manager also discusses results, plans and forecasts of the segment with the chief operating decision maker. [4]

Accountants aren't known for their imagination but here they are, proudly making stuff up. Are these standard writers really budding playwrights? Or will they soon publish a novel to bring to life their imaginary manager? In any event, the two boards play copycat in choosing the names of their fictional managers as the Chief Operating Decision Maker and Segment Manager, even if they do not have identical hypothetical functions.

Copycats but not quite complete cooperation.

[1] International Financial Reporting Standard 8, Operating Segments, IFRS 8, paragraph 5: An operating segment is a component of an entity:

(a) that engages in business activities from which it may earn revenues and incur expenses,

(b) whose operating results are regularly reviewed by the entity's **chief operating decision maker** to make decisions about resources to be allocated to the segment and assess its performance, and

(c) for which discrete financial information is available. (my bold text)

[2] Financial Accounting Standards Board, Accounting Standards Codification, ASC, 280, Segment Reporting, 10 General, section 5-3. (280-10-05-3)

[3] International Financial Reporting Standard 8, Operating Segments, IFRS 8, paragraph 9.

[4] Financial Accounting Standards Board, Accounting Standards Codification, ASC, 280, Segment Reporting, 10 General, section 50-7. (280-10-50-7)

They cannot agree on an accounting principle?

In the USA, accountants have 10 clear accounting principles they call GAAP: Generally Accepted Accounting Principles. In the UK and elsewhere, under IFRS Standards, accountants follow many of them too, except they do not believe they are accounting principles and call them something else.

In the UK, for instance, the FRC, which set UK standards for accounting, have invented 'pervasive principles': principles down in the detail, [2] completely different to the American principles. For example, in Section 8 of FRS 102, they state:

> "This section sets out the principles underlying information that is to be presented in the notes to the financial statements and how to present it."

The FRC do not classify these accounting principles as part of the foundation of accounting, as in the USA, but they classify them as principles in minor parts of accounting in the preparation of financial statements. They have principles for recognising and measuring inventories, one for recognising intangible assets, principles for amortising goodwill and many others. The FRC have changed some of the simple IASB standards into principles.

The IASB do not believe in accounting principles either. They have none. For instance in IAS 1, Presentation of Financial Statements, the word 'principle' does not appear. In their 'Conceptual Framework for Financial Reporting', they use the word 'principle' many times in the sense of 'in principle' and they mention some principles of communication, but no accounting principles.

Different name but same rules
In spite of not using the same word to describe these rules, principles or standards, whatever they decide to call them, eight of the 10 American accounting principles form part of the rules followed in the IFRS.

One of the 10 GAAPs is the Principle of Permanence of Methods. Procedures used to prepare financial reports must be consistent under this principle. The IASB must find the term 'permanence of methods' too American. They believe more in reliability and comparability in this context. Information, including accounting policies, must be presented 'in a manner that provides relevant, reliable, comparable and understandable information' (Paragraph 17b of IAS 1, Presentation of Financial Statements).

GAAP use the Principle of Sincerity. Sincerity requires financial statements to be accurate and impartial. The IASB do not agree with the sincerity of their financial statements. They use a different expression, 'faithful representation', which, according to them, means financial statements that are 'complete, neutral and free from error'. [3]

GAAPs not in IFRS

The two GAAPs not used by the IFRS are the Principle of Regularity and the Principle of Utmost Good Faith.

The principle of regularity states companies must adhere to GAAP. The IASB do not call this a principle, but do require companies to state that their financial statements adhere to IFRS standards. Similar but not quite the same!

'Utmost good faith' is a legal phrase with a long pedigree from the Latin term *uberrima fides* and is used today as a legal doctrine in insurance contracts to ensure full disclosure of all material facts. Using this long pedigree, the accountants who invented the Principle of Utmost Good Faith use it, perhaps, to force their fellow accountants to be honest.

Some GAAPs in accounting literature include the principle of good faith without the qualification 'utmost'. Is utmost necessary? Good faith on its own seems adequate. I cannot imagine two sets of financial statements for the same company with different results as a result of one being prepared with good faith and the other with utmost good faith. They must surely be the same with or without 'utmost'!

The IASB do not consider this principle necessary. You will note, however, that IFRS Standards use the word 'faith' in their rule above, that of 'faithful representation'. I find it odd that 'faith' in some form or another is important in both sets of standards, even if not always with 'utmost' or 'good'.

I would have thought accountants would have, what I call, the 'Padmé belief' in faith. Even if you are a Star Wars fan, you probably won't remember, in The Phantom Menace, the short exchange between Qui-Gon and Padmé, where she only has faith in what she can see and touch.

Faith is considered a belief and trust in God without total proof. Accountants live with facts and proof, so, omitting the religious part, they believe more in sight and touch, as does Padmé, the teenage Queen of Naboo. A pity the two boards don't explain their faith.

[1] GAAP: Understanding it and the 10 key principles, by Jason Fernando, 28th June 2022, https://www.investopedia.com/terms/g/gaap.asp.

[2] I didn't know the exact meaning of pervasive in accounting. The *Oxford English Dictionary* defines to pervade as: 'to pass into every part of; to spread throughout; to permeate; to saturate; to fill.'

[3] Conceptual Framework for Financial Reporting issued by the International Accounting Standards Board, paragraph 2.13.

ANNUAL REPORTS
Respect of material

You will remember, in the last chapter, I commented on 'true and fair' in audit reports. Well, auditors play another trick on us. They have an absolute true and fair and a qualified true and fair.

The vast majority of audit reports make the following statement, using the absolute true and fair:

> "In our opinion the Financial Statements give a true and fair view of the state of the Group's and of the Company's affairs …"

These are emphatic and to the point. But a few, and one has to search to find them, water down the 'true and fair' with the following statement:

> "In our opinion, the accompanying consolidated financial statements give a true and fair view IN ALL MATERIAL RESPECTS of consolidated equity and …"

These, of course, are my capitals. There is no effort on the part of these auditors to emphasise this qualification. They slip it in, I suppose, and hope that nobody, like me, will notice and comment on it.

What, I wonder, is the difference between a 'true and fair view' and a 'true and fair view in all material respects'? Should a shareholder worry about it? It doesn't sound the same: one is clear and direct, the other is watered down. But why?

Could it be that some immaterial statements have been included in these financial statements which don't make a difference, but should be highlighted? Readers are kindly asked to search for them.

If there is no difference, why put in the qualification? Auditors, after all, are intelligent, qualified people, and it cannot be an oversight. If the qualification is unnecessary, as I suspect it is, why not leave it out, instead of putting it in and telling us about it? And why do a few decide to include it?

Why is there a difference? Is it important? Perhaps it's a convention or another auditor's trick. Yet these same auditors in the same audit firm apply 'in all material respects' in their audit reports in USA, but not in the UK.

I suppose this relates to what I call the 'Starbucks syndrome'. When you buy a coffee in Starbucks, there is a warning on the paper cup:

"Careful! The beverage you are about to enjoy is extremely hot!"

You know it is hot, even extremely hot, because that's what coffee is and that's what you ordered. If it was cold you would complain, unless you ordered it with ice. Nobody reads the warning anyway. The writing is small and at the bottom of the cup. If you try to read it, you spill the coffee and burn your fingers. But the point, of course, is that customers are less likely to have a case if they were to burn themselves and think they could sue Starbucks for damages.

'In all material respects' is the same. You know the financial statements are presented fairly or true and fair because the auditors say so. That's what an unqualified audit report is all about. If there were minor errors, you wouldn't care. They are not significant. If there were material errors, the auditors would not state that the financial statements were presented fairly, would they?

They don't need to state 'in all material respects', yet they do, to show they are being open, prudent and clear with the reader, if they decide to read it, because, like the Starbucks warning, nobody ever reads audit reports anyway.

But it's not really a mystery; it depends where the directors register the company. Auditors reporting on companies registered in the UK follow the Companies Act and are not allowed to water down their true and fair with 'in all material respects'. These audits must be stronger and more complete that the others! And the others copy the Americans.

But some British companies do have 'in all material respects' in their audit reports. The International Consolidated Airlines Group (British Airways to the ordinary person), for instance, is registered in Spain, so their audit report does have the qualification, 'in all material respects'. So British Airways is not so British after all.

An invaluable value to worry about

The deferred tax asset is one of the least fun concepts invented in taxation and accounting. It's difficult to understand, difficult to calculate, and often a worry for the company and their auditors.

Accountants artificially reduce a company's losses by creating an imaginary tax credit called a 'deferred tax asset', which becomes an unrealisable asset in the balance sheet. You only need to note the words 'artificially reduce',' imaginary' and 'unrealisable asset'.

This happens when the tax authority in question accepts 'tax loss carry forwards' and only works if the company makes a profit in the future. How do accountants know whether there will be a profit in the future? They don't. They make a projection into the future showing a profit.

Accountants have created an asset based on estimated future profits. How unreasonable can you get? And still people believe that accountants are conservative and reasonable.

This imaginary asset then becomes a Critical Audit Matter for independent auditors, who have had to invent yet another concept, that of 'more likely than not'. Profits in the future, they say, are more likely than not to be created and management's future projections of profitability are reasonable according to their subjective judgement.

And, as usual, the accountants in the company are hard at work persuading the auditors to agree. Two is better than one. But is it enough? And what work do these two accountants do to come to this judgement? They consider all available positive and negative evidence. That is encouraging. What is this evidence? Taxable income, taxable losses and the projections. That's all there is. We are going in circles here.

Finally, after creating their imaginary asset, they have to test whether to 'write it down' each year, which, in normal language, means reduce its value. Accountants call this a 'valuation allowance'.

Two famous companies have massive deferred tax assets, Amazon and General Motors. Let's have a look at what they put in their annual financial reports.

Amazon

Amazon had $34.5 billion of deferred tax assets at the end of December 2022. [1]

The company worry about tax generally by including a paragraph entitled 'We Face Additional Tax Liabilities' in their risk factors, but do not mention deferred tax assets. The auditors also worry about what they call 'Uncertain Tax Positions' in their one 'Critical Audit Matter', without highlighting deferred tax assets. They do imply a concern when they make reference to notes 1 and 9, and state that 'there are many tax positions for which the ultimate tax determination is uncertain'. Uncertainty here could refer to deferred tax assets, but they do not specify.

General Motors

General Motors had $22.5 billion of deferred tax assets at the end of December 2022. [2]

The company worry about taxation with a paragraph in their risk factors. They use more alarming words than Amazon, for instance, 'Tax liabilities are subject to other significant risks and uncertainties.' Note the word 'liabilities' and not 'assets' and they do not refer to deferred tax assets. The auditors, however, do not worry, because taxes are not part of their Critical Audit Matters. All is well.

Worry is relative. I suppose that, more likely than not, future profits will compensate these deferred tax assets. We'll need to wait for the future to find out.

[1] Amazon Com, Inc, Form 10-K, Fiscal year ending 31st December 2022, Notes to Consolidated Financial Statements, Note 9 Income Taxes, page 64.

[2] General Motors Company, Form 10-K, Fiscal year ending 31st December 2022, Notes to Consolidated Financial Statements, Note 17 Income Taxes, page 89.

Accountants can't make up their minds

Accountants can't make up their minds on which risks to include in their annual reports.

Ability to attract: attractability

Out of the eight pharmaceutical companies I compared, six included the risk of not being able to hire and keep key employees, while two did not.

Six have statements similar to this:

> "The inability to attract and retain highly skilled personnel could ultimately impact our business or results of operations."

How come six companies in the same industry consider this a risk while the two others do not? They operate in the same countries, they cope with the same regulations and laws, they hire the same profile of employee, and yet two of them do not consider employee hiring and retention a major risk.

Abbott, for instance, do not have this as a risk, but in a section called 'Information with respect to Abbott's business in general' in their 2022 Form 10-K, they slip in a statement where they tell us that the sustainability of their business depends on being able to employ and keep not only people with diverse backgrounds, but, more important I guess, talented people. So it is not a material risk for Abbott, but it needs to be brought to the attention of the shareholders.

The other is GSK. They have no employee hiring or retention risk. They are able to attract and retain highly skilled personnel in their headquarters in Brentford, UK, yet AstraZeneca would appear to be struggling to retain employees in their headquarters in Cambridge, only 70 miles away! How odd!

Perhaps GSK made a mistake omitting it, but they state otherwise. In their 'Key Performance Indicator' section, they show one on employees: 'Top talent and succession plans for key roles', which they mark as 'n/r – Not reported externally due to commercial sensitivities'. GSK are so proud of these plans that, first, they announce a KPI, then, cheekily, give no results, and finally, they know that with this plan, they will not lose their top talent, so there's no risk. The reader, though, has to search around for the reason hidden away in their report.

Taxation

Everybody has to pay taxes, so taxation is business as usual, but some companies consider taxation a risk. They worry about potentially negative consequences from changes in, or interpretations of, tax laws, and how they might affect the results of operations, cash flows and financial condition.

But Johnson & Johnson go much further than others. One has to wait until the last sentence of their tax risk section to become worried. [1] Here they say that their tax treatment could be different to that of the tax authorities, which in turn could mean that their tax estimates are insufficient. Perhaps there is a problem in their tax department, or they have ongoing tax audits that are not following expectations. Something seems to be happening, but we are not sure what. Otherwise, why would they include this risk? But the key to this issue may come from the following statement:

> "The Company conducts business and files tax returns in numerous countries and is addressing tax audits and disputes with many tax authorities." [1]

Could it be that other companies do not have tax audits and disputes with many tax authorities? Or with fewer disputes, they have a reduced risk? But how many disputes and tax audits does a company need before the risk should be included in their annual report? Or is it the amount disputed that is a risk? But this is not indicated. Perhaps the others have efficient tax departments. The very mention of this risk creates more questions than answers.

The danger of taxation policies is to think too far out of the box; some companies 'think out of the tax'!

[1] Johnson & Johnson, Form 10-K, Fiscal year ended 1st January 2023, Risks Related to Government Regulation and Legal Proceedings, page 11.

Foreign currency

Some companies consider foreign currency a risk but not others, whereas currency movements are the way of life they have chosen, and another business-as-usual excuse to add to risk statements.

Six companies in my review – Abbott Laboratories, AbbVie, Bristol Myers Squibb, Johnson & Johnson, Novartis and Sanofi – follow this policy and consider foreign currency a risk, with statements such as:

> "Fluctuations in foreign currency exchange rates may adversely affect the company's financial results and its ability to realise projected sales and earnings." (My wording.)

There are two companies that do not agree to having a foreign exchange risk.

AstraZeneca do not mention currency in their risk overview, though they admit that they cannot influence currency exchange rates, which have affected the results of their business, and they insist that currency movements are 'outside the company's control'. Yet they do admit to foreign currency risk and exposure, but not in the risk overview. They have a dedicated paragraph called 'Foreign currency risk', where they tell us that the US dollar is their most significant currency, so they manage exposures against the US dollar, as well as presenting their results in this currency.

GSK agree and have a 'Foreign exchange risk management' section as part of their financial review and a 'Foreign exchange risk' paragraph in their notes to financial statements, without a mention in their 'Principal risks and uncertainties'.

So perhaps they own up to a foreign currency risk, but do not consider it material enough to include it in their risk overview? Perhaps they forgot to put it in? We will never know. However, they have declared it, even if one has to read the whole report to find it.

Unfortunately, there is no obligation for companies to explain why they do not identify as a risk something that other companies consider a risk. Readers of annual reports have to search for the reasons. But not all missing risks have their absence explained.

Integration

Seven of the pharmaceutical companies have acquired companies in the recent past. They have all turned these opportunities into risks. They must have known the risks and estimated their capacity to integrate them before making the acquisitions, but still concluded that the anticipated synergies and benefits from the acquisition outweighed those risks. Yet as soon as they were acquired, the four announced a material risk in the annual report.

> "AbbVie may not be able to integrate acquisitions successfully into its existing business."

Abbott use the same wording as AbbVie, but also worry about additional debt and unknown liabilities. Sanofi do not worry about how successfully they integrate their acquisitions, but how quickly and efficiently.

Bristol Myers Squibb are alone in questioning their ability:

> "Our ability to successfully integrate Celgene and MyoKardia could impact our results of operations."

Now I don't want to quibble about the use of English (which is what the book is essentially about), but what Bristol Myers Squibb are trying to tell us is either 'If it turns out that we don't have the ability to successfully integrate …' or 'Yes, we have the ability, but if we screw it up …' I guess it must be the second; they would never admit that they do not have the ability to integrate Celgene and MyoKardia, or they would never have taken on the project.

AstraZeneca are frustrated that an ineffective integration of Alexion may mean targets are not met, or that it may damage their brands and even their financial position or results.

Novartis write the following:

> "Failure to identify, execute, and/or realize the expected benefits from our external business opportunities."

Johnson & Johnson also worry about benefits, but more specifically strategic benefits and the time it might take to achieve them. They are the odd company out because they did not seem to make any material acquisitions during the year, yet still referred to a risk relating to acquisitions. This may be because they insist on the longer term strategic benefits from acquisitions in previous years.

GSK did not carry out any material business acquisitions in 2021.

We are back to the 'if unsuccessful' syndrome and to business as usual. Their business is to integrate their acquisitions. If they cannot then they should not acquire them.

The rubber-stamp UKEB

Most accountants don't know (and perhaps don't care) that the UK no longer needs to follow new accounting standards issued by the IASB. And why? Because of Brexit.

So the United Kingdom Endorsement Board, or UKEB as it is now known, was set up to 'influence, endorse and adopt new or amended international accounting standards'. The key word here is 'amended'. The UKEB has the power to change International Financial Reporting Standards (IFRS), applicable to the UK.

So what are they going to do? They don't come out and say. They have issued their 'Regulatory Strategy', which doesn't mention IFRS. But in their introduction, they use this rather odd expression that they establish themselves as 'as the UK's voice on IFRS', which I guess implies that they will follow IFRS.

But will they follow them without change? The ICAEW worry. They wrote in their representation letter on this same 'Regulatory Strategy':

> "We nonetheless believe that any divergence with IFRS as issued by the IASB should be avoided wherever possible."

And they go on using diplomacy to make their point with force, but as politely as possible:

> "Experience suggests that the full benefits of IFRS adoption can only be reaped if the standards are adopted in FULL."

(These are my capitals for 'full', not the ICAEW's. I sense, when reading the paragraph, they want it in capitals, in italics and in bold characters, but, as they are polite accountants, elegance prevails.)

While reading, I wondered what the point of the UKEB could be, if their job is simply to adopt the standards in full. No point at all, you might say. But the board have been given the power to change the standards if they want. They can now influence, endorse and adopt at their will.

The UKEB's first act was to adopt IFRS 17 Insurance Contracts in full without changes. [1] They took 184 pages to decide, to show what they did and to explain why. Their conclusion, too, was interesting. According to the UKEB, IFRS 17 goes much further than the mere objectives of the standard of 'improved financial information'. It 'meets the criteria of understandability, relevance, reliability and comparability required of the financial information needed for … assessing the stewardship of management.' [2] How about that!

Now I am not sure what 'stewardship of management' means, nor what criteria management require to assess it. Perhaps I will read the report in its entirety to find out. But I digress.

I am happy, however, that they came to this conclusion without making any changes. John Stokdyk of *accountingWEB* agrees with me:

> "It's probably better for everyone concerned that the UKEB pursues the rubber-stamp path rather than interfering radically with what has passed through the IFRS mechanisms." [3]

And he concludes his article using this wonderful phrase that warns of 'a mishmash of international standards' if endorsement boards worldwide become too 'active'. We already have a double mishmash with the disagreement between the FASB and the IASB. If the UK go out on their own, we'd have a triple mishmash, which would take financial reporting back to the last century by not following IFRS. We would then have three sets of accounting standards. How long will it take before this happens?

[1] Paragraph 12, IFRS 17 Insurance Contracts, Endorsement Criteria Assessment issued by the United Kingdom Endorsement Board, May 2022.

[2] Stewardship of management as well as this whole sentence is part of Regulation (EC) No 1606/2002 of the European Parliament and of the Council of 19 July 2002, and you will find it in Article 3. The UKEB seems to think it is important in spite of the UK no longer being part of the EEC.

[3] Article in *accountingWEB*, UK Endorsement Board stirs into life, by John Stokdyk, 6th September 2022.

Material marks on the bench

What do accountants do when regulators forget to make rules? They create collective chaos. And justify it with aplomb. Or, put simply, they go crazy. I am reluctant to reveal the subject matter in this chaos because it is so serious and so boring. I'm bored myself thinking about it. I even reworded the title to hide it. So bear with me a little longer.

The situation arises when legislators in the UK put in a clause forcing auditors to explain in writing how they use their professional judgement. This only happens in the UK. Nowhere else in the world are auditors required to make these detailed explanations, so they never do. They simply announce that they have used their professional judgement.

In the UK, however, auditors are required to reveal how they fix materiality limits. So from a list of the 50 largest UK-based companies, I chose two companies audited by each of the four largest audit firms, and, in the table below, I list what they call their materiality benchmarks. There is one remarkable constant: none use the same base.

MATERIALITY BENCHMARK

Adjusted profit before taxation.
(Ernst & Young, Associated British Foods)

Normalised Group profit before taxation.
(KPMG, Unilever)

Adjusted profit before tax from continuing operations, including net pension finance costs.
(Deloitte, Tesco)

> Three-year average of the Group adjusted operating profit before tax attributable to shareholders' profits from continuing operations.
>
> (PricewaterhouseCoopers, Aviva)

> Statutory profit before tax, Adjusted profit before tax, Revenue and Net cash flows from operations.
>
> (Deloitte, GSK)

> Adjusted EBITDAaL.
>
> (Ernst & Young, Vodafone)

> PBTCO normalised to exclude this year's investment and other variances and losses attributable to non-controlling interests.
>
> (KPMG, Legal & General)

> Profit before tax after adding back intangible asset impairment charges (Note 10), fair value movements and discount unwind on contingent consideration (Note 20), the discount unwind on the Acerta Pharma share purchase liability (Note 3), material legal settlements (Note 21), the unwind of the fair value adjustment to Alexion inventories (Note 2) and restructuring charges relating to the Post Alexion Acquisition Group Review (Note 2).
>
> (PricewaterhouseCoopers, AstraZeneca)

The auditors make each as different as possible, even within the same accounting firm. It is as though they compete against each other for complexity. If so, PricewaterhouseCoopers win in their audit of AstraZeneca.

But there are some similarities. All use profit as their base, but never the same profit. All adjust their profit, most of them agreeing on the word 'adjusted', with two exceptions. KPMG prefer 'normalised', whereas PricewaterhouseCoopers use the expression 'adding back'. Only PricewaterhouseCoopers with their 'adding back' tell us what they adjust the profit by. The others leave it to our imagination.

Having made their choice of benchmark, auditors must explain that choice. Their explications go from the delightful to the weird and sometimes even with an attempt at humour.

Delightful
My favourite is Deloitte's in their audit of GSK. Statutory profit is what Deloitte delightfully call 'metrics used by investors and other readers of the financial statements' (whoever they may be), which makes it all the more justified to use as a benchmark.

They claim that 'statutory profit' is a recognised and important metric used by investors and readers of financial statements. But only Deloitte use it! It only comes up in their audit report. In the other annual reports, there are statutory tax rates, statutory allowances, statutory deadlines, even a statutory audit fee, statutory auditors (of course) and many other statutory items, but never statutory profit. What an important benchmark!

Innovative
The most innovative is Ernst & Young in the Vodafone audit with their Adjusted EDITDAaL. Please note the 'Adjusted' with a capital A. Adjusted by what? They do not explain. Now most people, even accountants, have no idea what EBITDAaL means, let alone Adjusted EDITDAaL. For the ignorant like me, EBITDAaL represents EBITDA after Leases. This has recently become fashionable in some industries, and as Ernst & Young state, it 'provides us with the most relevant performance measure on which to determine materiality given the prominence of this metric …' Of course! Everyone knows EBITDAaL covers materiality so much better than EBITDA.

Trendy
The trendiest is KPMG in the Legal & General audit, with 'PBTCO normalised'. Nobody ever uses PBTCO. If you don't know, PBTCO represents profit before tax from continuing operations. KPMG choose the trendy accounting method of using initials instead of stating what they mean, yet we all know they are competent auditors, so there is no need to show off in this way.

Serious and weird

PricewaterhouseCoopers are both the most serious and weird. They are alone in choosing a three-year average with Aviva. I wonder why. Profits must be jumping around, so to keep their percentage and the materiality amount stable, they have decided to average. But of course they don't tell us.

The weird benchmark, invented by PricewaterhouseCoopers in their audit of AstraZeneca, belongs in a chapter I didn't write, The Ludicrously Complicated. Its only merit is clarity and seriousness; they explain every adjustment in mindboggling detail, which their colleagues don't. And then they claim, but surely tongue in cheek, that 'these amounts (add backs) are prone to year on year volatility and are not necessarily reflective of the operating performance of the Group', so must be excluded from the benchmark calculation. Of course, they must add it back!

Another constant

In this chaos there is, however, another constant. All of them believe their chosen benchmark is the best, the most relevant from which to choose the materiality limit. They emphasise their independence and show their originality in auditing, or as they all state somewhere, they apply their 'professional judgement'. What they don't say is that the application of their professional judgement can create chaos.

Percentage

The auditors do, however, almost converge on the percentage that they choose to calculate the materiality limit. The favourite is 5% and percentages close – 4.8%, 4.7% or 4.6% – in six out of the eight companies.

KPMG own up to having an internal guideline for fixing a maximum materiality limit in their Unilever audit report:

> "When using a benchmark of Group profit before taxation to determine overall materiality, KPMG's approach for public interest entities considers a guideline range of up to 5% of the measure."

However, KPMG do not believe in rounding up to 5%; they consider 4.8% and 4.7% to be more accurate, whereas PricewaterhouseCoopers consistently choose 5%, but with different profit bases.

There are two exceptions to this 5% rule. Ernst & Young go wild with a lowly 2% in Vodafone but justify and explain nothing. I guess they felt worried by 5%, which would have meant a high materiality limit of €725 million, giving them little audit work to carry out. With GSK, Deloitte are alone in choosing an amount, in this instance £210 million, as their materiality limit 'using professional judgement', which they then measure against their unknown statutory profit before tax, giving 3.7%.

Accountants might be boring, but if you leave them without rules to follow, they adore chaos and are quite happy to explain it using delightful, trendy, innovative and weird explanations.

[1] From a list of the 50 largest UK-based companies, I chose two companies audited by the four large audit firms PricewaterhouseCoopers, Deloitte, Ernst & Young and KPMG from the 2022 annual reports of the companies named above.

FORMAL REPORTS
Rollover the iron curtain

Iron curtain as an accounting adjustment – I found this silly. Why not call it 'cold war'? Equally silly. I tried to find the origin without success. Perhaps the Soviets invented it. But the Securities and Exchange Commission (SEC) officialised the method and the title in their 'Staff Accounting Bulletin 108' in 2006, so it cannot be them.

Accountants at the SEC recognise it as one of two 'techniques most commonly used in practice' to correct material misstatements in financial statements. Commonly used by whom, I wonder. I had never heard of it, no doubt because I am not in the habit of making material misstatements in my financial statements. Accountants who make these mistakes must know them well, and probably their auditors do too.

But why iron curtain? The adjustment must hide something, and it does. The prior year financials are wrong and never corrected. Could this be the reason?

The second of these techniques, to quote the SEC again, is 'generally referred to as' rollover. This is another counterintuitive term not related to accounting. I'd never heard of this one either. And 'generally referred to' by whom? Rollover to most accountants, at least those who work in investment, usually refers to the transfer of funds from one investment to another, often between retirement funds, with no relation to accounting errors.

In one of their accounting examples, they make this rather surprising statement:

> "The staff believes that this can be accomplished by quantifying an error under both the rollover and iron curtain approaches."

The staff here are the accounting specialists working at the SEC. They recommend accountants use both techniques at the same time. Logical, because the iron curtain method corrects the balance sheet, and the rollover corrects the earnings statement.

My title, Rollover the iron curtain, should perhaps have been 'Iron the curtain, then roll it over'. Both silly.

Royal Charter

The Institute of Chartered Accountants of Scotland trumpets their 'chartered' more than any of the other institutes, because they were the first to be granted a Royal Charter, receiving it from Queen Victoria back in 1854. Chartered has nothing to do with boats or contracts; it is a Royal privilege, and with it comes a beautiful style of writing.

The Charter starts with this magnificent phrase:

> "VICTORIA R VICTORIA, by the Grace of God of the United Kingdom of Great Britain and Ireland, Queen, Defender of the Faith, to all to whom these presents shall come, Greeting:"

And continues with an introduction of nearly 500 words before giving her okay:

> "… And the Petitioners thereby humbly prayed that We would be graciously pleased to grant them a Royal Charter, incorporating

them, and such persons as may hereafter be duly admitted Members, into one body corporate and politic, by the name, style and title of THE SOCIETY OF ACCOUNTANTS IN EDINBURGH."

'We' here is, of course, Queen Victoria and, back then, the organisation was not yet an institute but a 'society', and not for the whole of Scotland, only Edinburgh. This city has the privilege of starting off the 'chartered fashion', which many institutes have chosen to copy.

Queen Victoria seems to have been an avid supporter of accountants as she granted another charter to the English and Welsh some years later, followed by the Irish in 1888.

Being chartered gives them so much more respectability, credibility and above all nobility. Chartered accountants are noble. Queen Victoria declares she is 'satisfied that the intentions of the Petitioners are laudable, and deserving of encouragement ...' What praise back then and even today.

Not to be outdone, Queen Elizabeth II granted a charter to another set of accountants in 1974, the ACCA, the only body of accountants to be both certified and chartered, combining the noble with the mad. They decided not to become an institute but an association.

Chapter 3

Amusing Fun

JARGON
A BIT of an E – an EBIT

Now, why would accountants calculate a profit, reverse a portion, give it a name, and then not include it in financial statements?

Companies do not include EBIT in their financial statements because they don't use it as an internal measure of profitability. Accountants outside the company use it to compare the profitability of different companies. So some accountants use EBIT, and only some of the time.

In addition, EBIT is not recognised by accounting standards, so in theory EBIT does not officially exist. And because it doesn't exist, accountants do not have a standard way of calculating it.

But what is it? For most experts, EBIT = net profit + interest + taxation. But accountants cannot agree on whether the interest expense is just that, or whether it should also include other related expenses, for instance, currency gains or losses on the interest-bearing loan.

In March 2017, the IASB did start a discussion at one of their public meetings by presenting a 'Staff Paper' on EBIT, asking whether it should be included in financial statements. [1] I don't know if anyone ever responded, or cared enough to respond, but I do know that EBIT is still not part of international standards.

In the earnings statement, accountants could highlight EBIT to reach their net earnings. But no, that would be too logical and too easy. Let's make it more complicated and calculate it separately or not at all. And let's not agree on how to calculate it.

So we still have an accounting term widely used by accountants, but not part of the official financial statements, vital for understanding the profitability between companies, with no recognised definition, where readers of the said financial statements are required to calculate it on their own.

And you thought accountants were logical, methodical and clear with numbers. Not with EBIT! And not with EBIT's Yorkshire father (Da) EBITDA either.

The DA in EBITDA is not DA at all

Every accountant knows that EBITDA = EBIT + depreciation + amortisation. But it is still without an official definition. EBITDA has rather taken over, as if he were EBIT's overbearing elder brother, and he does appear in some financial statements. So I thought I would have a look at seven well-known companies' financial statements and see what they say about EBITDA.

Amazon, GSK and Johnson & Johnson do not have EBITDA in their annual reports. Roche, in their 2021 annual report, support my claim that EBITDA is not used by companies as a measure in their financial statements:

> "The Group does not use ... EBITDA in either its internal management reporting or its external communications."

But they cooperate with their readers and continue with:

> "For the convenience of those readers who do use EBITDA, this is provided in the table below."

And they give a calculation by business segment of EBITDA (at least for the two years). How generous of them.

The auditors alone mention EBITDA in the Walgreen Boots 2021 annual report, as part of their discussion of Critical Auditing Matters. They bring in what they call 'EBITDA margins', whatever they might be, requiring 'a high degree of audit judgement'.

AstraZeneca like EBITDA the most, with 15 mentions in their annual report and they have a calculation they call a 'reconciliation' to help their readers.

Associated British Foods like EBITDA too. They sprinkle it around their 2021 annual report five times. They even calculate it in Note F to the financial statements and include an impairment charge in their EBITDA calculation.

Associated British Foods give us the proof that the initials EBITDA are incorrect. The DA in EBITDA should be replaced with DAI, taking on the Welsh (even Japanese) given name meaning beloved. It should be EBITDAI: Earnings before Interest and Taxes and Depreciation and Amortisation and Impairment. EBITDA is a myth without the 'I' for impairment.

But accountants have an answer to my irreverent comments. They argue that companies do not always have impairment charges, but certainly do have both depreciation and amortisation. So they think their DA is correct most of the time. And that is good enough for them.

[1] IFRS, AP21A, Staff Paper, Paper Topic Earnings before interest and tax (EBIT), March 2017, https://www.ifrs.org/content/dam/ifrs/meetings/2017/march/iasb/primary-financial-statements/ap21a-pfs.pdf.

Accounting inputs

How unimaginative can you be! The IASB fail miserably in IFRS 13 with their new accounting term 'inputs'.

Instead of giving complicated names as accountants usually do, they introduced Level 1 inputs, Level 2 inputs and Level 3 inputs in this IFRS standard. This lack of imagination is, I suppose, useful because it is quite impossible to guess what they could mean without reading the standard.

But the IASB are not alone. The FASB have the same terminology – Level 1, 2 and 3 inputs – in the same context, that of establishing fair value. Therefore, the two boards must have consulted to make this lack of imagination a worldwide accounting phenomenon.

They both call them inputs, but they are not inputs or values, they are 'prices'. Now why would they call inputs 'prices'?

If you don't believe me, these are their definitions:

> "Level 1 inputs are quoted prices in active markets …"
> (IFRS 13 Definition)

> "Level 1 inputs. Quoted prices (unadjusted) in active markets …"
> (Taken from the Glossary of FASB Accounting Standards Codification)

But then, by the time inputs get to Level 3 they are no longer 'prices' but are 'unobservable inputs'. Again, both accounting boards use the same term. So why didn't they call them 'unobservable prices' or Level Zero inputs (because there are none), instead of 'Level 3 inputs'? I don't know! To confuse us or to keep it, at least, logical – number 3 comes after number 2!

But they make it even more confusing. How about this – an observable input is developed using publicly available market data, whereas for an unobservable input, i.e. a Level 3 input, there is no market data available, and it has to be invented by the users of the standard.

How about that for a surprise: if there is no market data, what else can accountants do except invent something themselves?

Trigger happy

I found 'trigger' in several annual reports. Not, as you might guess, in the sense of pulling the trigger of a gun, because none of the annual reports related to gun manufacturers. Companies often use it in the sense of 'to cause or bring about'.

Sanofi for instance uses it in its simplest non-accounting form when they announce that the invasion of Ukraine was triggered by the Russian invasion.

I found that AstraZeneca trigger the most, and use it in the most complicated way:

> "We perform a rigorous impairment trigger assessment for all our intangible assets."

I don't know what a rigorous impairment or a rigorous trigger is. And I am not sure whether they mean an 'impairment trigger' or a 'trigger assessment'. I guess AstraZeneca don't either. It would seem, therefore, that they have invented a new accounting buzzword – the 'impairment trigger assessment' – which they perform rigorously for all their intangible assets. Other companies merely test intangible assets for impairment.

And AstraZeneca trigger other complicated actions. They trigger regulatory milestone payments, sales-related milestones, development and regulatory milestone payments, and the entitlement to cash-severance arrangements. Plus they have set trigger points and trigger events from time to time. So AstraZeneca find triggering a popular activity in their company.

But my champion in trigger expressions goes to Kroger Co., who manage to trigger activities more than 20 times.

In the context of clinical and regulatory milestones, I found this complicated sentence where triggering seems important to them:

> "There can be significant uncertainty over whether it is highly probable that there would not be a significant reversal of revenue in respect of specific milestones if these are recognised before they are triggered due to them being subject to the actions of third parties." [1]

But read this amazing sentence, which, in seeking to convey what they do as part of their 'Key Compensation Practices', explains that they:

> "Double-trigger change in control provisions in all equity awards beginning in 2019." [1]

Well, now we know!

I guess only the employees of the company know what this means, and I suppose they are happy with the double trigger. If it means doubling salaries, they certainly would be happy. But I guess an equity award is receiving shares in the company without paying for them. If, however, it means doubling the number of conditions or controls to be eligible for the award, employees might be less pleased.

But they also have another compensation activity called, would you believe, the 'single-trigger acceleration'. They define it in this complicated way as 'automatic acceleration of vesting of equity awards upon a change in control of the Company'. How lucky the employees are!

Other companies have simpler trigger actions. They trigger uncertainty, they trigger competition and one even triggers licences. But triggering is not such a popular activity. Wiser companies never tell us when they pull the trigger, nor whether they even have one at all.

[1] The Kroger Co., for the fiscal year ended 29th January 2022, Notice of 2022 Annual Meeting of Shareholders 2022 Proxy Statement and 2021 Annual Report on Form 10-K, pages 57 and 93.

STANDARDS
Two to tango

As Mr Barckow, the head of the International Accounting Standards Board, said in an interview with the *Wall Street Journal* published on 6th September 2021, while talking about harmonisation of accounting standards, which he calls 'convergence':

> "Reviving convergence is not imminent. Obviously, it takes two to tango."

Both the FASB and the IASB have manoeuvred themselves into a position of verity. They are both reviewing the accounting standards around goodwill, and they both state they want harmonisation of accounting policies, and yet they are not talking to each other about goodwill, at least not publicly.

It is simple common sense to harmonise the rules now that they have both decided to review them at the same time. By talking together, they could put aside their differences and agree on a common standard on goodwill that would benefit the financial world. But I would suggest that common sense is not on the agenda.

Forget the tango – the two boards are not listening to the same music. In fact, they are not even in the same dancehall. Perhaps one has defected to Morris dancing (with their headquarters in the UK). Anyway, neither has invited the other to dance.

They are moving towards divergence, not convergence. It seems that the FASB wants to amortise goodwill and the IASB wants the status quo without amortisation. I'm not sure that the two boards even realise that they would leave themselves open to some ridicule if they came up with different rules on accounting for goodwill in the next few years.

By September 2023, the IASB had only got as far as publishing an exposure draft, so there is still a long way to go. At the beginning of 2024, both boards are still working on the subject. It must be very difficult to decide. It seems, though, they are still not dancing together.

I look forward to their decisions and the chance to write about which dance they choose. A tango is too fast – a waltz would suit them better. After all, it takes two to waltz, but a whole troop to pull off a good Morris dance.

The two boards' intellectual evolution

You will have recognised by now that I complain endlessly about the lack of cooperation between the FASB and IASB. But I have stumbled on the concept of 'faithful representation'.

The first time I saw it was in the IASB's Conceptual Framework, when this sentence caught my eye:

> "To be a perfectly faithful representation, a depiction would have three characteristics. It would be complete, neutral, and free from error." [1]

Surprising, I thought, the word 'faithful' is unusual for the IASB. Faith, you will remember, is part of the 10 GAAP in the US. The last one is the Principle of Utmost Good Faith. Has the FASB, I wondered, brought pressure on the IASB to include some faith in their standards?

So I started reading the FASB's Conceptual Framework to see what they thought about 'faithful representation'. I had to plough through to Chapter 3 to find this sentence in paragraph QC 12:

"To be a perfectly faithful representation, a depiction would have three characteristics. It would be complete, neutral, and free from error." [2]

THE TWO SENTENCES, ONE FROM IASB, THE OTHER FROM FASB, ARE IDENTICAL!

This is not cooperation, I thought, not so much taking two to tango, but dancing in perfect synchrony.

And then I discovered the two boards agree on many parts of their Conceptual Frameworks. It must be why they chose the same name. What a surprise.

But what is this concept of faithful representation? In my day as an accountant, financial statements had to be reliable. Reliability included three elements: substance over form; prudence; and verifiability. I made sure financial information was reliable, prudently preparing the essential, i.e. the substance, making sure I could verify my numbers. But this is no longer good enough for today's accountants.

The boards replaced reliability with 'faithful representation' and gave it three characteristics: complete, neutral, and free from error. They replaced substance over form with complete, prudence with neutral, and verifiability with free from error.

I tried to understand what they are trying to do.

It is true that substance over form implies completeness but doesn't state it, and verifiability is a long way from being free from error. But accountants should not worry too much because 'free from error does not mean perfectly accurate in all respects'. So free from error is not perfect, but perfect is free from error. I have no idea how close the two have to be when making an accrual or an estimate.

But the boards do try to explain this concept to us, with this affirmation: an accounting estimate doesn't have to be free from error, if it is faithful. It is faithful if you explain clearly how you made the estimate. If that is not splitting hairs, I do not know what is.

Neutral, though, is interesting. The boards decree that prudence is now biased, and accountants must no longer be prudent but neutral. With this change, I would expect overall results of companies to improve because prudence means lower income and higher expenses compared to neutral. This is true in the USA, but not in the rest of the world. The IASB disagree by stating:

"Neutrality is supported by the exercise of prudence."

The two boards are not in agreement on the definition of neutral. What a surprise!

Remember, in my time, accountants prudently prepared the substance, making sure they verified their numbers. Now they faithfully prepare neutral depictions, free from error. Surely this makes financial statements more accurate?

And then I wondered why, all of a sudden, the two boards were strolling hand in hand with their similar Conceptual Frameworks. And then I remembered, their frameworks are not standards. Accountants do not have to follow them. They are not important, so agreeing is easy!

[1] Conceptual Framework for Financial Reporting issued by the International Accounting Standards Board, paragraph 2.13.

[2] Financial Accounting Standards Board, FASB, Statement of Financial Accounting Concepts No. 8, Conceptual Framework of Financial Reporting, Chapter 1, The Objective of General Purpose Financial Reporting, and Chapter 3, Qualitative Characteristics of Useful Financial Information, August 2018, paragraph QC 12.

The madness around probable

Accountants take the word 'probable' and give it two different meanings depending on where they live. How mad is that?

Let's first look at what the *Oxford English Dictionary* thinks of the word. This presumably is what the non-accountant believes it should be. They define 'probable', in the context of this accounting event, as something which can 'be reasonably expected to happen', [1] and then they mess it up by adding 'likely'. They define likely 'as having a high chance of occurring', [2] so we end up with an accounting event that is BOTH reasonably expected to happen and has a high chance of occurring.

This is not possible for an accountant. 'Probable' is either 'reasonably expected to happen' OR 'a high chance of occurring', not both. One would expect them to choose one or other of these two definitions for their future accounting event. But no, even that is too simple.

The two accounting boards agreed to disagree on the definition of the word 'probable'. However, they did agree that it should be different to the *Oxford English Dictionary*'s definition. How devious and complicated can accountants get? But that is the situation today. The FASB put their definition in ASC 450 and the IASB in IAS 37.

'Probable' for the FASB, under US GAAP means 'likely to occur'. For the IASB probable means 'more likely than not'.

Accountants now agree that the IASB definition of 'probable' has a lower threshold than under US GAAP, and in practical terms accountants give 'more likely than not' a greater chance than 50%, and 'likely to occur' a greater chance than 75%.

To summarise:

> IASB probable = more likely than not / more than a 50% chance
> FASB probable = likely to occur / more than 75% chance

The word 'probable', then, has different meanings under IASB and FASB. Same word different meanings! Can accountants be boring when they do this?

So what? You might ask. Let's take a simple sentence that could be in any annual report:

> "A liability is recorded when a loss is probable and can be reasonably estimated."

Now, in a company reporting under IFRS, this would mean that an accrual would be made when there was a 51% chance or more that a liability would occur. Whereas under FASB standards, this same accrual would be made when there was a 75 % chance or more that a liability would occur.

Let's take some actual examples from financial reports. The word 'probable' occurred 26 times in the Johnson & Johnson 2021 annual report issued under US GAAP and 32 times in the GSK 2021 annual report under IFRS reporting rules. Both used 'probable' in their commentary on legal disputes.

The auditors of both companies used the word 'probable' in their opinions: once in the GSK audit report relating to how they apply materiality, and seven times in the Johnson & Johnson 2021 annual report relating to litigation. On average, the European pharmaceutical companies used the word 'probable' 39 times and US companies 30 times.

And they use 'probable' in many different situations. Here are three:

> "Deferred tax assets are only recognised where it is probable that future taxable profit will be available to utilise losses."

Future profits have more than a 50% chance of happening under IFRS standards, whereas under US GAAP, future profits have to have more than a 75% chance before a deferred tax asset would be created.

> "… when it is probable that all contractual payments due will not be collected …"

Here under US GAAP the company only has a 25% chance of getting paid, but under IFRS standards it has a 50% chance. Now it is difficult to estimate these percentages, but I prefer a statement like this in Europe where payment is more likely.

> "… and the sale is probable within one year of the reporting date."

In this statement for a company in the USA the sale is more certain to happen, less certain in Europe.

The two boards cannot agree on the meaning of the simple word 'probable'. As a serious accountant, I wouldn't know whether to laugh or cry at the level of absurdity of this situation. As a fun accountant, I can laugh about it.

[1] *Oxford English Dictionary*: Probable. a. Having an appearance of truth;

that may in view of present evidence be reasonably expected to happen or be the case; likely. Now the usual sense.

[2] *Oxford English Dictionary*: Likely Probable. 2.a. In predicative use with anticipatory it as subject and that-clause as complement: having a high chance of occurring; probable. Also in it is likely or as (it) is likely, used parenthetically.

A trusted global language worldwide

I wondered whether I could have some fun with the IASB's mission statement. And, surprise, surprise, I found things to muse about even in the first sentence.

> "Our mission is to develop high-quality IFRS Standards that bring transparency, accountability and efficiency to capital markets around the world."

They want their standards to bring transparency, accountability and efficiency to capital markets. Good for them! Had they exchanged financial markets with financial statements, they would have been more accurate, but one can argue that accurate financial statements bring efficiency to capital markets. And this is a mission statement, so mentioning capital markets is nobler than the more mundane term 'financial statements'.

Transparency means following the standards, declaring accounting policies and revealing information that is material for the users of the financial statements. And the auditors are there to make sure that all this information is revealed.

Accountability and efficiency are more difficult to prove. When a company chooses to follow accounting standards, or is required by law to adopt them, the directors become accountable. They, after all, have to declare that they follow the IFRS standards.

One can debate whether standards bring efficiency. Efficiency is the performance of a task with little effort or time. The mission statement proclaims that the standards make financial markets more efficient. They might *help* to do that, but it's still an exaggeration. Or are they talking about preparing financial statements? But users of financial statements don't care if they've been prepared efficiently, only that they are accurate. (See the full mission statement of the IFRS below.)

Second sentence
Here is their second sentence:

> "Our work serves the public interest by fostering trust, growth and long-term financial stability in the global economy."

I find this extravagant. Okay, their standards are used in 140 countries, but not in the USA or China, [1] the two largest economies, so 'global' is an exaggeration. A 'significant part' of the global economy would be better, but still an exaggeration.

This statement tries to convince us that accounting standards foster growth in the economy. Now, they might foster many things, especially for accountants, such as extra work, more responsibility, complexity and additional risk of being sued, but not economic growth. Perhaps they have a team of people circulating the world talking to governments with the slogan:

> "Adopt our standards to foster economic growth in your country."

Who would fall for that?

Moreover, not only do accounting standards apparently foster growth, but the IFRS also claim their standards foster 'long-term financial stability'. Take note: not just financial stability but long-term stability. This claim makes me speechless. Or more precisely 'wordless'.

Now, if we take these two exaggerated claims out of the statement, it doesn't read quite so well:

> "Our work serves the public interest by fostering trust in 'a significant part of' the global economy."

This is more accurate, but it doesn't sound very encouraging as a mission statement.

My favourite phrase

But my favourite phrase comes under their mission statement, on the same page of their website (https://www.ifrs.org/about-us/who-we-are/), under the heading 'IFRS Accounting'. Here the IFRS claim their standards are a 'trusted global language worldwide'.

It comes in this sentence:

> "The Standards have in effect become **the** global language of financial statements—trusted by investors worldwide …" (My bold text for 'the' – they could have written 'a' global language or 'one' of the global languages.)

I have moved the words around to make it punchier, but the trusted global language worldwide is what this sentence claims. The metaphor becomes poetic, standards are an accounting language, but they don't recognise the FASB language. If the IFRS standards are the trusted accounting language, what are the FASB's? A foreign accounting language not to be trusted?

And note the IFRS repeats the word 'global': global language and global economy. I will not conjecture why.

FASB mission

Given the flowery IASB mission statement, I had a look at the FASB's version to see what they think.

You will notice the FASB mission is sober. [2] It includes nothing about financial markets or the global economy, and it makes no reference to transparency, accountability or efficiency. They develop or foster nothing. And words like trust, growth and long-term financial stability are absent. All they want to do is to improve financial accounting reporting and give us useful information. They then explain how they do this: by encouraging, participating and considering.

The IASB has a flowery mission statement, the FASB a sober one.

IFRS mission statement
"Our mission is to develop high-quality IFRS Standards that bring transparency, accountability and efficiency to financial markets around the world. Our work serves the public interest by fostering trust, growth and long-term financial stability in the global economy."

IFRS Accounting
"Since its creation in 2001, the IFRS Foundation has transformed the global landscape of financial information by introducing IFRS Accounting Standards developed by the International Accounting Standards Board (IASB). The Standards have in effect become the global language of financial statements—trusted by investors worldwide and required for use by more than 140 jurisdictions. We are continually developing and improving the Standards."

[1] Chinese accounting standards are based on IFRS Standards, but the Chinese authorities have altered some.

[2] In March 2024, I asked the FASB for permission to reproduce their mission statement. Their reply was ambivalent, where they informed me that reproduction would be 'an acceptable use'. This gave me hope, but they spoiled it by adding 'we would grant permission'. They didn't give me permission, but **would** grant it, without informing me of the conditions under which permission would be given. Given this dubious wording, I have not reproduced it, but you can find it here: https://fasb.org/about-us/facts.

You may remember that the FAF oversees the FASB. Do not be confused by the FAF's different mission, which you can find on this page: https://accountingfoundation.org/about-us/about-the-faf. It is similar but different, while remaining as sober as the FASB's.

Note that the FASB and the FAF don't have mission statements, just missions alone.

ANNUAL REPORTS
Fun statements from annual reports
In this section, I note entertaining phrases and sentences I found in reading annual reports.

General Motors: leveraging

"This all-new platform is flexible and will be leveraged across multiple brands and vehicle sizes, styles and drive configurations…"

"We will continue to leverage our architecture portfolio to accommodate our customers."

"… leveraging our experience with remote work …"

General Motors like leveraging and use it often. But why? It makes me think of cars being winched up in workshops so they can be looked at underneath or the car jack used to raise the car to change tyres on the side of the road after a puncture. They obviously concentrate on car sales and don't want to be open about repairs and breakdowns, but leveraging is clearly a subliminal reminder not to forget to service your car!

And they like 'societal':

"We believe that building all-electric vehicles with autonomous capabilities integrated from the beginning, rather than through retrofits, is the most efficient way to unlock the tremendous potential societal benefits of self-driving cars."

'Tremendous potential societal benefits', how sophisticated.

And General Motors are oh so ambitious:

"Our vision for the future is a world with zero crashes, zero emissions and zero congestion …"

Clearly this is a figurative ambition, quite impossible to achieve and in total contrast to the down-to-earth 'leveraging' throughout their annual report. They should go the whole hog and add zero repairs, zero punctures, zero breakdowns, and why not zero cash while we are on this track? Free cars.

bp: trading inventories

"Trading inventories are valued using the quoted benchmark prices adjusted as appropriate for location and quality differentials. They are predominantly categorised within **level two** of the fair value hierarchy."

They are mentioning the inputs without stating 'inputs'! 'Level two of the fair value hierarchy' is a Level 2 input described earlier. Quite apart from assuming the reader knows in detail the different elements of this IFRS standard, I am not sure what the 'They' in 'They are' refers to. Is it the 'trading inventories', the 'benchmark prices' or the 'quality differentials'? It must be the benchmark prices. Remember, I told you inputs are prices for the IFRS.

> *Legal & General Group: inclusive capitalism*
> "Our purpose is to improve the lives of our customers, build a better society for the long term and create value for our shareholders – we call this inclusive capitalism."

'We call it' means you can redefine anything you like: 'Here's a huge grey animal with a trunk, tusks and big ears – we call it a bicycle.' Or 'A payment as protection against unforeseen circumstances – we call it a rip-off.' Legal & General Group seem to have reinvented an 'inclusive capitalism' for themselves, together with their own definition. For people who know the usual meaning, Legal & General imply they help the poor. Those who have never heard of inclusive capitalism might believe Legal & General's definition is the universal one.

> *Legal & General Group: levelling up*

They are so forward looking and trendy that they do things not only before they were invented, but long before, and they boast about it:

> "We were doing 'levelling up' **long** before the phrase was invented ..."

> *Unilever: step-up and pivot*

Unilever are into step-ups. They 'step-up in operational excellence'. Their strategic focus 'has contributed significantly to the step-up in performance'. They 'have worked hard to step-up' their brands and execution in markets 'over recent years'. They have 'a winning strategy, one that is backed up, operationally, by a considerable step-up in the quality' of their execution in the marketplace. And, finally, their financial director states that '2022 saw a step-up in growth …' and a 'step-up in brand and marketing investment'.

These are not all the step-ups in their annual report, but there are so many, it will become monotonous if I continue. They must be trying to demonstrate the health of their company by getting their 10,000 step(up)s in or perhaps they are competing with uplift!

As well as stepping up, Unilever pivot; unfortunately, only twice, but pivot they do. They continued on their 'journey of pivoting the portfolio' and then rather dramatically their 'historical societal trends' continue 'until 2030, then rapidly pivot'.

Sadly, they don' tell us on what they pivot, how quickly they pivot or the result of their pivoting. I am sure we would find it entertaining if they did.

Taxation in AbbVie

"Prescription drug manufacturers such as AbbVie are also subject to taxes …"

Of course they're subject to taxes. What is the point of telling us this?

Bristol Myers Squibb: the longest sentence

The prize for the longest sentence in the world from annual reports must go to Bristol Myers Squibb with 570 words. I am not allowed to reproduce the sentence in this book without their permission, and if I ask them, I am sure they would not give it to me, given the imaginary prize I suggest. You will find it on page 24, the second paragraph of their 2021 Form 10-K, and on the URL below. [1] I checked the equivalent paragraph in their 2023 Form 10-K and they have taken out more than 100 words. (P.S. I have not read either in full, and I doubt anyone else ever has either.)

Other risk statement verbiage

"The strategy includes leveraging our personnel's experience and making societal impact a key driver of our employees' engagement."

I have no idea how to make societal impact influence the engagement of employees in any company, and I certainly don't know how they would leverage it either. And to place this vague action into the strategy of the company overwhelms me. But I must be alone.

EPS and Tesco
"Our adjusted diluted EPS rose by +88.8%."

Tesco don't highlight EPS (earnings per share), they calculate something more complicated: adjusted diluted EPS. They then even admit that it 'is presented on a basis other than in accordance with IAS 33'. So it is not in accordance with accounting standards.

When I read statements like this, I automatically think, what are they trying to hide? This time, my first thought was not quite so excessive. It was first 'Okay, Tesco must like the 88.8% increase', so they emphasise it, and second, 'What is the rise in the real EPS, the one which is not adjusted or diluted?' I couldn't find it. However, I must admit I got fed up going back and forth in the pages of the report searching for their definition of adjusted and diluted.

Copying legal disclaimers
These three companies are being sued but don't want to give us the details, so they write these almost identical sentences in their annual reports. I don't know who is copying whom, but here they are:

AstraZeneca
> "We do not believe that disclosure of the amounts sought by plaintiffs, if known, would be meaningful with respect to these legal proceedings."

GSK
> "The Group does not believe that information about the amount sought by plaintiffs, if that is known, would be meaningful with respect to those legal proceedings."

Novartis
> "Plaintiffs have alleged claims in these matters and the Group does not believe that information about the amount sought by plaintiffs,

if that is known, would be meaningful with respect to those legal proceedings."

[1] https://annual-report.bms.com/assets/bms-ar/documents/bms-2021-10-K.pdf page 24, second paragraph.

Accounting madness of Plavix

Back in 2021, Reuters published an article entitled:

> "Bristol Myers Squibb, Sanofi ordered to pay Hawaii $834 million over Plavix warning label." [1]

The article explained how the two companies had engaged in unfair and deceptive business practices for more than 10 years.

I was fascinated to find out how the two companies reported and recorded the penalty in their financial statements. Bear in mind that the judge considered the liability of the two companies to be equal, so he apportioned a 50% penalty to each company.

Bristol Myers Squibb explained the issue as one of 'labelling, sales and/or promotion of Plavix', [2] or, in my words, a lack of adequate labelling and poor promotion. Sanofi explain things more clearly by paraphrasing what the Hawaii AG (Attorneys General) alleged; namely that Plavix did not work well for patients with certain generic backgrounds and the two companies did not disclose this information.

However, when it comes to the accounting treatment of the issue, Bristol Myers Squibb's approach is clear, while Sanofi's is like a puzzle that requires digging to figure out.

Bristol Myers Squibb remained confident in their appeal, given the merits of their case, and did not believe they needed to establish a reserve for this matter. So they made no provision for $417 million despite the court's decision.

Sanofi explained the judgement but did not state whether they had made a provision or not. However, in the introduction to the note 'Legal and arbitral proceedings', they did make the following statement:

> "In the cases that have been settled or adjudicated, or where

quantifiable fines and penalties have been assessed, we have indicated our losses or the amount of provision accrued that is the estimate of the probable loss." [3]

The court had ordered Sanofi to pay a penalty of $417 million. This would surely have settled the case and enabled Sanofi to calculate the penalties. But they appealed. They went on to say in part B 12 that they record provisions when they have a present obligation.

They don't state clearly that they have made a provision and they don't say whether they consider this court order **is** a present obligation. I conclude it is and, with these statements from their annual report, that Sanofi have made a provision of $417 million for this case.

If this is true, we are in a position of two pharmaceutical companies being jointly prosecuted and jointly judged, but only one of them takes a $417 million charge in their financial statements. This I call accounting madness.

If this is not true, only Bristol Myers Squibb is clear in what they have done; Sanofi remains fuzzy.

In the end, they both should have made a provision. In May 2024, the court awarded the state $458 million from Bristol Myers Squibb and $458 from Sanofi. They will no doubt record these amounts in their 2024 annual reports.

[1] Reuters, Bristol Myers, Sanofi ordered to pay Hawaii $834 million over Plavix warning label, by Tina Bellon, Nate Raymond, 16th February 2021, https://www.reuters.com/article/us-bristol-myers-sanofi-plavix-idUSKBN2AF1YI.

[2] Bristol-Myers Squibb Company, Forms 10-K, for the fiscal years ended 31st December 2021 and 2022.

[3] Sanofi, Form 20-F, for the fiscal year ended 31st December 2022.

Difficult FRC risk management

The FRC 2021 risk management section is a classic example of how **NOT** to write one. It is so full of amazing jargon and mumbo jumbo that I recommend you look it up on their website. [1] I find it entertaining and I hope they leave it up for many years. Unfortunately, someone in the organisation had the same opinion as I, and changed it to normal English in their 2022 annual report. What a shame, but the 2021 report is still there at the time of writing this book.

The FRC, as you know, controls the accounting profession, including, as its name suggests, financial reporting, so one would expect that their report would be anywhere close to perfect. I must commend the 2021 report as a model of clarity, thoroughness and transparency **except** for the risk management section, which remains as verbose as ever and is full of incomprehensible statements. They start with 'risk appetite', which I still find amusing, even if this term is now a recognised and much-used expression in risk management, and is included in many annual reports. Risk appetite is supposed to be the amount of risk an organisation is willing to accept. But they don't tell us how big their appetite is, nor what they want to eat.

Here is the first odd statement:

> "We have conducted de-escalation processes and risk identification sessions …"

By the time I reached 'sessions' I was thinking of what I would be doing at the weekend, and had to start again. I'm not sure how to 'conduct' a process. I can start one, design one, follow one but conduct one? Do I need a baton to wave? I have no idea what a de-escalation process is either. De-escalating what? They mention emerging threats, so perhaps this is relevant.

And when I found this sentence, it stopped me in my tracks:

> "We have stress-tested plans by horizon scanning internal macroeconomic and event-driven scenarios such as climate-related risks and enhanced business continuity plans." [1]

My goodness! What impressive adjectives to explain scenarios! How can anyone write a sentence like this and stay credible? I wondered what they were trying to say, so I went back and had a look. Let's try to analyse what they are trying to tell us that is so important, it needs to be included in their annual report. As I am a mere accountant under the control of the FRC, their report is supposed to be relevant to me.

I could accept this:

"We have stress-tested plans by scanning scenarios such as climate-related risks and business plans."

Although stress-testing 'plans by scanning scenarios such as business plans' doesn't make that much sense either. And then why is horizon scanning better than scanning on its own? Horizon here could mean long term. But perhaps not – one can never reach the horizon. Could this be relevant? Or are they becoming poetic, by leaving it to the reader's imagination to decide what it means?

Okay, so they only scanned internal scenarios or, more specifically, the internal macroeconomic ones. They clearly feel the need to be specific. This must be relevant. External scenarios were not scanned, and definitely not external microeconomic ones. Presumably, they are not relevant.

But it's not over yet. They considered event-driven scenarios. Now I'm not sure whether they are 'internal' event-driven scenarios or all the event-driven scenarios – and that worries me. Have they covered everything? But then I don't understand what an event-driven scenario is. Does anyone outside the FRC?

And finally, I will comment on 'climate-related risks'. I am unable to imagine what type of climate-related event could affect the workings of the FRC. Perhaps lightning striking the building and burning it down? They do not specify. But if it is that important, they should tell us what they mean, and not leave us in this precarious limbo, wondering how they spend their time and what real risks they are trying to explain to us.

I could go on with their concern of risks and scenarios around business plans. But I will spare you as this is becoming too ludicrous. If you know what they are talking about, please let me know.

Now to be fair to the FRC, their annual report for the year ended 31st March 2022 was substantially improved by someone having taken a red pen to many of these weird expressions. However, they still revert to odd words from time to time. For instance, their risk management framework 'has recently been refreshed'. An odd word to use in this context, but creative. But it doesn't stop there. They refresh things 10 times in their report, for instance, they will be 'refreshing the FRC website', they have refreshed 'communications strategy' and 'security tools', and, my favourite, 'a refresh of the values and behaviours'. Fresh values and fresh behaviours! Does that mean they are squeaky clean, or they need not be washed before dinner?

In addition, they continue to drop in some of the ludicrous expressions inherited from their 2021 report. For instance, they '**embed** a positive risk culture', and they 'oversee the effective **cascade** and **escalation** of information'. A waterfall of information crashing down on stakeholders' heads and drowning them in content and jargon, then escalating back up on the moving staircase, miraculously revived!

Later in the risk management section they do come to their senses and revert to normal risk management English:

> "… we have continued to enhance and improve our risk management framework to identify and manage risks that may prevent us from delivering our strategy …" [2]

Embedding, cascading and refreshing have vanished. What a relief! I guess, at this rate, I will have nothing to write about in their latest annual report.

[1] Financial Reporting Council, Annual Report and Financial Statements for the year ended 31st March 2021. https://media.frc.org.uk/documents/FRC_Annual_Report_and_Accounts_2020-21.pdf.

[2] Financial Reporting Council, Annual Report and Financial Statements for the year ended 31st March 2022. https://media.frc.org.uk/documents/FRC%20Annual%20Report%20and%20Accounts%202021/22.pdf

Don't worry, HMRC is here to stay

I read with astonishment the audit report of HM Revenue and Customs (HMRC) for the period ending 31 March 2023, with this heading:

> "Conclusions relating to going concern".

HMRC will never go bankrupt, so why does the auditor make a

statement on going concern? Should we be worried? Well, no. The auditor does not 'cast significant doubt on HM Revenue and Customs' ability to continue as a going concern ….'. It seems that going concern in this context does not mean that HMRC could go bankrupt, but that their services will 'continue into the future'.

But Gareth Davies, Comptroller and Auditor General, is more precise. He states that HMRC will continue 'within a period of at least 12 months'. Has he received assurances from government to make these two extravagant statements? 1) HMRC is able to continue as a going concern, and 2) HMRC will continue for another 12 months.

Having successfully collected net revenues of £543.1bn in 2022 and a further £611.1bn in 2023, why, I thought, would the government disband HMRC after 12 months? Further, to quote strategic objective number 4, it is 'a great place to work' for the more than 66,000 staff. They even have a dedicated group of 'Chief People Officers', which 'develops and oversees implementation of HR policies that make HMRC a great place to work'. How relieved they must have felt when they read the audit report, telling them they had a job for at least the next 12 months.

It must be that the auditor, Gareth Davies, is using his audit judgement to state the obvious. He considers they're going to keep on collecting tax for at least the next 12 months. And his message is important enough to inform readers of the report, whoever they might be, that HMRC will be in existence next year. He doesn't actually state this either but his 'no significant doubt' expression must be part of his judgement too. Let's be prudent.

I have no reason to question that HMRC prepares financial statements on a going concern basis (not principle), which is a legal requirement, but the rest is ridiculous. They can be prepared on this basis without insisting they will still be there next year.

Deliberate distraction

The FRC include a deliberate distraction in one of their risk statements, or is it an innocent oversight? Here it is from their 2021 annual report:

> "Corporate reporting and audit quality remains inconsistent, resulting in in material misstatements in some accounts, resulting

in reduced investor/stakeholder/public confidence and reputational damage to the FRC." [1]

Did you see the typo? Two ins: 'in in material misstatement'. Now I don't want to be polemical but what does this say about the FRC? It's true, I didn't notice it in my first read. I caught it when I copied the sentence into my Word document and the second 'in' was underlined in red. A clear and obvious mistake? Or could it have been put there on purpose because any proofreader would pick this up easily? Perhaps there wasn't a proofread in this section? After all, who reads the risk management section of any annual report, except proofreaders?

But if it was put there on purpose, why? Perhaps to take attention away from the seriousness of the perceived risk? Now, why would I make this ridiculous claim that it was put there on purpose? It's a typo and an insignificant typo at that!

This is because I have my own story about a deliberate grammatical error left in the previous book I wrote, proposed by my proofreader. It came in a contract-type document, where I was using formal legal language and made the mistake. The contract was a silly one and I was trying to be funny by keeping the text serious. My proofreader suggested that we keep the mistake to highlight the humour. I agreed.

So we had a little fun in keeping a grammatical error as a mistake or as an attempt at humour, which nobody ever noticed. A moment of lightness in a tedious job of proofreading.

Despite the typo, this is an extraordinary statement. The impact of this risk, they say, is high and it is likely (4 on a scale of 5) that, in the future, some corporate reports will show material misstatements not picked up by the auditors. How's that for the quality of reporting in the UK? Not only this, but also it will likely damage the reputation of the FRC. Wow!

But why worry? The FRC come up with three solutions, which they pompously call 'mitigations', to this massive problem of reporting and auditing:

"FRC increasing intensity of its forward-looking supervision of the major audit firms."

Not supervision alone, but forward-looking supervision, whatever that entails. Are they congratulating themselves before the event?

And then comes:

> "Failures to comply with standards are identified and referred as appropriate for Enforcement action."

What does 'enforcement' with a capital E mean? A second typo, or because Enforcement is Really Important? They don't explain it in the annual report. They assume you know the difference between Enforcement actions, Enforcement procedures and their Enforcement Division. They even assume you know AEP, the Audit Enforcement Procedure. The FRC use this incomprehensible jargon to show how they investigate and punish auditors for substandard work.

The third solution is as follows:

> "We revise standards based on feedback drawn from FRC monitoring and enforcement work, to address failures or poor quality."

I would hope they do revise the standards when necessary, but it takes so long that the reputation of the FRC would already be lost.

[1]   Financial Reporting Council, Annual Report and Financial Statements for the year ended 31st March 2021, page 44, Risk number 3.

Worry about worrying

The directors of Abbott Laboratories Inc. worry about the level of their debt:

> "Abbott has significant indebtedness, which could adversely affect its business, including decreasing its business flexibility."

As of December 31, 2021, Abbott's consolidated indebtedness was approximately $18.1 billion.

Nothing special about this. Let them worry.

The directors of Bristol Myers Squibb also worry, but they don't worry as much, even though their debt is more than twice that of Abbott, because of the acquisitions of Celgene and MyoKardia. They worry that their flexibility to invest, to develop new products and to pay dividends may be reduced.

The Bristol-Myers Squibb Company's consolidated indebtedness was $44.6 billion.

However, the company that worries the most is AbbVie, and so they should. Their debt on 31st December 2021, including the current portion, was $76.0 billion, more than four times the level of the worried Abbott Laboratories Inc. This debt, they say, could adversely affect their business and their ability to meet their obligations.

Worriers

Bristol Myers Squibb worry only about their reduced financial flexibility. Abbott worry about their ability to 'raise additional financing', even their ability to make scheduled payments with respect to indebtedness and, above all, about their credit rating.

AbbVie's list of worries, as you might imagine, is long. They take on the worries of both Abbott and Bristol Myers Squibb and add a few more. They worry about their cash flow and their ability to make interest payments. They worry about the future of their company, that they 'may not be able to borrow money, sell assets, or otherwise raise funds on acceptable terms, or at all, to refinance' their debt.

I guess if the directors of Abbott Laboratories Inc. were transferred to AbbVie, they would have an immediate heart attack. They worry with a debt of $18.1 billion, so they clearly could not operate with a debt of $76.0 billion. On the other hand, you can imagine how thrilled the directors of AbbVie would feel if transferred to Abbott. They would borrow a quick $58 billion in a flurry of spending to get up to the debt level they like working with.

But the directors of AbbVie don't just worry about the debt they have; they finish by worrying about the debt they intend to incur:

> "The amount of debt that AbbVie has incurred and **intends to incur** could have important consequences to AbbVie and its investors."

I guess shareholders should worry about this too. As a simple solution, I would recommend they stop worrying about the 'debt they intend to incur' and not incur it! That would be a quick way to reduce worry and lower their risk!

MAGAZINE ARTICLES
Tweaking accountants
I was amused by this secondary headline from the *Wall Street Journal*.

> "Finance chiefs say they have had to tweak their forecasts ..." [1]

I remember revising forecasts as a CFO, but never tweaking them, nor twisting or jerking them. And perhaps in the USA, CFOs might yank a forecast, whereas in Britain they would pull one. Twisting a forecast has the connotations of dishonesty and so must be put aside. I would contend that, as accountants, we are serious and do not tweak forecasts – we revise them.

To be fair, the serious meaning of tweak means to make a minor adjustment. But here, too, I beg to differ. If I have a forecast that requires a minor adjustment, then I wouldn't bother to change it. I only adjust a forecast if I need to change it significantly. American accountants might tweak forecasts, and British ones adjust, revise or change them, but never tweak.

Still, the sentence reads better with 'tweak'. 'Revise' is too formal. It is, after all, more fun to tweak a forecast than to revise it!

And then I had another surprise. Not only do accountants tweak forecasts, but they tweak goodwill. I discovered an article in the *Wall Street Journal* with the following headline:

> "FASB Approves Tweak to Goodwill Accounting Rules for Private Companies, Nonprofits" [2]

Okay, so it is an old article, published on 10th February 2021, and applies to private and non-profit companies in the USA, but it is not so much the content but more the word 'tweak' yet again that caught my eye. I never tweaked forecasts and I can't imagine how accountants can tweak goodwill.

As we've seen, tweak usually means a small adjustment. Nobody is going to make a small adjustment to goodwill. If an impairment test on goodwill comes out slightly below the book value, a small adjustment will be made to the impairment test to improve it, so that no adjustment is necessary.

But then I couldn't help noticing that my first impression when reading the headline was wrong. I realised that the tweak was to the rules of reporting not to the value of goodwill. Private companies have more time to make their impairment tests in the USA than before.

That was the tweak that was not!

[1] *Wall Street Journal*, How CFOs Set Their Outlooks Amid Waves of Virus: One Day at a Time, by Kristin Broughton and Mark Maurer, 18th October 2021.

[2] *Wall Street Journal*, CFO Journal, FASB Approves Tweak to Goodwill Accounting Rules for Private Companies, Nonprofits, by Mark Maurer, 10th February 2021.

Chapter 4

Surprising Fun

JARGON
Jargon is back
From the simple word 'back', accountants invent two of the most surprising financial terms.

The first is 'bounce back'. The British government designed what they called the 'Bounce Back Loan Scheme' to support businesses during the Covid pandemic. As well as its surprising name, the design and implementation of the scheme by the Treasury was equally surprising. Or, according to the minister in charge at the time, Lord Agnew, 'nothing less than desperately inadequate'. [1]

And further, during the oversight, it seems that the relevant actors were asleep:

> "If only BEIS (Department for Business, Energy & Industrial Strategy) and the British Business Bank would wake up …" [1]

But I am digressing. In an attempt to mask the name and their implementation troubles, they reverted to using the initials BBL. But BBL also means Bounce Back Lenders, so confusion continues. Bounce back, whether accountants like it or not, is now part of their jargon, regardless of whether they hide it away in the initials and regardless of whether the government forced it upon them.

The second financial term using back is 'claw back'. Not crawl back or craw back, but still a horrible term. The *Oxford English Dictionary* says 'clawback' was first used as a noun in 1549 to describe 'one who claws another's back; a flatterer, sycophant, parasite, "toady."'

The *Oxford English Dictionary* quotes the *Daily Telegraph* in 1969 in the financial use 'It … is necessary to adjust the claw-back for …'. Since then, accountants, in the UK anyway, have adopted this ancient word in its *Daily Telegraph* meaning with enthusiasm.

It now means a reimbursement or repayment, but when using claw back the emphasis is usually on the difficulty incurred in achieving the said reimbursement. It is most often used in taxation, but one can claw back almost anything today: expenditure, losses, prices, even territory when used with Ukraine.

But imagine my astonishment when I discovered an article on *accountingWEB* with both terms together 'BBL Claw Back'. [2] Naturally, the author, on this serious subject, could not have entitled his paragraph 'Bounce Back Loan Claw Back'. Too frivolous! And two words 'Back' in the same title would be a distraction. BBL Claw Back has a better ring.

But who knows what a BBL Claw Back is anyway? I checked on Google and obtained this stunning sentence:

"KCorp and BBL claw back in VCT EMEA in Week 5." [3]

Google had not seen the article in *accountingWEB*. It turns out that BBL here is BBL Esports, a Turkish team which plays in video game competitions on Riot Games, and, would you believe, was ranked 36th in Europe in April 2023.

So there you are!!

[1] Resignation Statement in the House of Lords over Coronavirus Fraud made by Lord Agnew on 25th January 2022.

[2] Article in *accountingWEB* by Will Cole on 3rd July 2023, 'Essex bookkeeper banned as director over Covid-19 loan abuse'. https://www.accountingweb.co.uk/tax/business-tax/essex-bookkeeper-banned-as-director-over-covid-19-loan-abuse.

[3] https://www.vlr.gg/204776.

Nothing standard about standard costing

Accountants call it standard costing but there is nothing standard about it! Standard signifies something common, but only the method is standard. Accountants agree on more than one standard without agreeing on how many. Some accounting textbooks say there are two types of standard costing, others three, a few five or more, with terms such as ideal, basic, current, expected and normal standards. Accounting literature on standard costing is vast.

To call it standard costing and then declare up front that there are three or more different types is, as usual, accountants being complicated. They then go on to explain that the standards have major weaknesses. Some of these are so serious that companies do not use them.

The most popular accounting theory agrees on three types of standard costing. The Institute of Certified Public Accountants in Ireland, for instance, claims these three exist:

Basic standard costs
Ideal standard costs
Currently attainable standard costs [1]

Basic standard costs do not change over many years. The advantage of this type of standard is that it provides a base for comparison with actual cost over a period of years. However, changes will occur over time, rendering the standards useless, because they do not represent current costs and variance analysis but merely explain differences against the time the standards were set.

Ideal standard costs assume 100% efficiency and no idle time (a short trip to the toilet or a cigarette outside during working hours or just a pause for daydreaming). These standards are not used in practice because they tend to demote the staff using them with their persistent negative variances. To overcome this weakness, some companies set standards as goals to aim for rather than the perfect performance. This now makes not three but four different standard costing methods!

Currently attainable standard costs should be attainable under efficient operating conditions. These standards incorporate the possibility of machine breakdowns, normal wastage and lost time. Accounting theorists generally recommend this method of setting standards, which just proves that there are as many standard costs as companies that use them. 'Attainable' in one company does not mean the same as 'attainable' might in another.

Thus accountants not only make the theory of standard costing complicated but also mislead the world with the term 'standard', for there are millions of standards, as many standards as there are companies using them. Accountants should not call the method standard costing but infinity costing.

[1]   CPA Ireland Standard Costing by Rosemarie Kelly, Examiner F2 Management Accounting.

STANDARDS
The mysterious event in the past

'As a result of past events' appears in the definition of an asset, a liability and an obligation. I am writing rubbish, you might say, but the IASB defines an asset as follows:

> "An asset is a present economic resource controlled by the entity as a result of past events." [1]

Not only do we not know what the event was nor what happened at it, but they announce them in the plural. They need more than one event to create an asset. Further, this asset is no longer an asset without these past events. Most peculiar!

I tried to find out if anybody had discovered what these past events were. Nobody seems to know and I couldn't find a precise definition. It appears that the event depends on the asset and the transactions relating to it. But they only explain ONE event, whereas the definition states there must be at least two!

The IASB are not alone. The FASB use a similar phrase in their definitions of asset and liability: '… as a result of past transactions or events'. They are more precise with their word 'transactions'. An accountant can assume that a past transaction must be made between two companies for an asset to be placed in the financial statements. This seems logical. But then they spoil it by adding 'or events'. Again, why more than one? Why no explanation of what an event might be?

Did they collaborate or copy each other? I don't know who decided first and who copied whom, or perhaps the two accounting boards had a meeting to decide the importance of these past events, and to agree to include them in their respective definitions. They must have agreed not to explain them either.

Then, in December 2021, the FASB had a change of heart. They eliminated past events from their definition of an asset and a liability. [2] One can reasonably assume, they state, that a present right was obtained from some past transaction or event. Not only did they confuse their fellow accountants with plural transactions and events, but they admitted that there was only ONE event.

Then they concluded, with unusual force, that the phrase '… as a result of past transactions or events' was redundant.

The IASB do not agree. They continue to believe that accountants must assume a present right was obtained from past events in the plural, without any attempt to explain what they are. They remain mysterious, unknown and unexplained.

[1]   International Accounting Standards Board, The Conceptual Framework for Financial Reporting, Paragraph 4.3.

[2]   FASB Statement of Financial Accounting Concepts No. 8 Conceptual Framework for Financial Reporting, Chapter 4, Elements of Financial Statements, December 2021, Appendix B: Basis for Conclusions, Assets and Liabilities, BC4.13.

Rotten food

Rotten food stays in companies' inventories and accountants give it a value. Fresh food recently purchased is sold first, leaving rotten food on the shelves. This, anyone would agree, is laughable. But accountants value inventory this way in the food industry in the USA with the last in, first out (LIFO) method. If the latest purchase is the first thing sold, then old inventory stays in the company. I have always found this method intellectually challenging.

It is no better in the oil industry, which calculates the physically impossible. The old oil cannot be separated from the new (first out) in any tank. Yet accountants separate them in the financial statements, leaving old inventory, LIFO, in place indefinitely, perhaps purchased more than 100 years ago.

And to make it worse, accountants publicly recognise that LIFO inventory valuation distorts financial results. Books and articles have been written about it for more than 30 years. One of them concludes:

> "Our study provides evidence that the use of the LIFO inventory accounting method by oil companies results in significant accounting information distortions in inventory turnover, gross profit, working capital, and current ratio." [1]

And yet the auditors of these companies blatantly state that the financial results are fairly stated. But then, they have to do this because US GAAP allows LIFO inventory valuation. So here we have an official accounting standard knowingly distorting financial results. There are, of course, reasonable accountants who lobby for change. They have an irrefutable argument: the USA is alone in the world. Their rival, the IASB, does not permit LIFO valuation in their standards.

But when a system has been in place for so long and when its main objective is to reduce the tax bill for companies, resistance to change is considerable. The additional tax payable for each company would be massive.

Further, many institutions would have to agree not only to abandon LIFO valuation but also to invent a method of transition. This is difficult, given the number of institutions involved: the SEC, the tax authorities, the FASB, and others. In addition, many companies use LIFO inventory valuation. It is estimated that 15% of companies in the S&P 500 use LIFO. [2] And this is without counting on the lobbying power of the large US oil companies.

So accountants knowingly defend the illogical and allow distorted financial statements, in flagrant breach of their stated principles and values. Next time you buy a bar of chocolate, hope that the company is not running down inventory – it might be 20 years old!

[1] *Journal of Accounting and Finance* vol. 14(5) 2014, LIFO and Accounting Distortion – The Case of the Oil Industry, by June Li and Megan Y. Sun, University of Wisconsin, River Falls.

[2] In 2021, approximately 15% of companies in the S&P 500 used LIFO as their primary inventory method and 50% used FIFO, according to Credit Suisse Group AG, citing annual reports.

A close member of the family

Would you believe accountants define exactly what they consider to be a close member of the family?

All this is part of what they call a 'related party'. Now, of course, when we hear the word 'party', we usually think of a birthday bash or a night out with friends eating and drinking. A party here is either a person or an entity. It is difficult to choose a word that describes both a person and a thing, so they choose 'party' to make it sound fun. But let's stick to the person part for the moment.

'Related' here has nothing to do with a family unit, but to the 'person … that is related to the entity that is preparing its financial statements'. [1] And then they go on to inform us that this person is not alone; they come with part of their family:

> "A person or a close member of that person's family is related to a reporting entity if …" [1]

Now this is where IASB define a close member of the family. To keep it simple, accountants believe that children and the spouse (as they call them) are close members of the family, or the 'domestic partner'. They do not go into any detail about what a domestic partner actually is. I wonder why they don't include brothers, sisters or grandparents.

The FASB use the same accounting term – related parties – but instead of 'close members of the family' they use the term 'members of their immediate families'. [2] Immediate family become related parties only when they control or influence. The family members that don't control or influence an owner or manager are not related parties.

But without stating who influential people are, I cannot imagine auditors interviewing family members to determine whether a particular member influences another, but this is what they imply, because they give no examples.

Brothers, sisters, grandfathers and grandmothers are NOT close members of a family according to the IASB. If you are an accountant, you are never close to your brother, sister or any grandparent, so keep your distance.

[1] International Accounting Standard 24, Related Party Disclosures, IAS 24, Paragraph 9.

[2] Financial Accounting Standards Board, Accounting Standards Codification, ASC, 850, Related Party Disclosures, 20 Glossary.

Poetry, not only in standards

In the likely event that you have not read IAS 37, [1] I must show you the first part of the definition of a 'constructive obligation'. Their attempt at poetry is quite spectacular.

Here is the section:

> "A constructive obligation is an obligation that derives from an entity's actions where: a) by an established pattern of past practice, published policies or a sufficiently specific current statement, the entity has indicated to other parties that it will accept certain responsibilities; and …"

Look at those five p's: 'pattern of past practice, published policies'. Who would ever write a sentence with five consonants in poetic juxtaposition in such a serious document? They are clearly out to create a poetic whole. (Or do I mean a poetic hole in this context?) But that is not all. Notice how they include assonance with the four a's in 'established pattern of past practice'.

Without shame, they follow it with another alliteration, this time with three s's: 'sufficiently specific current statement'. And then I wonder, did they intentionally slip in another assonance with their three u's in published, sufficiently and current.

The sentence, of course, is incomprehensible. But it is, at least, interesting to read, if only because of these poetic literary devices to entertain and distract the reader.

How about this, in the IASB's Conceptual Framework in their attempt to define 'understandable'?:

"Classifying and characterising information clearly and concisely makes it understandable."

On the other hand, I find the FASB disappointing. Their poetic prowess rarely ventures beyond a little alliteration and occasional assonance. There is a rather dull sentence in ASC 250-10-05-3 that manages to include 'entities may be enhanced' and end in a flourish with 'careful consideration', while sprinkling the two letters 'p' and 'c' throughout the sentence.

And here is another, a timid use of alliteration with the letter 'm' in their explications of going concern:

"... management's plans, when implemented, will mitigate ..."
(ASC 250-40-50-7)

I did also find this rather bold: 'The amount recognised reflects a reasonable expectation...'. But that was all.

None of these can be unintentional. Writers of the standards must each have a rogue colleague in their midst who manages to slip in these poetic elements to distract or amuse the reader. But they are so rare that even the editors and proofreaders must have found them. But, of course, we will never know what infelicities the editor or proofreader may have brought to the author's attention, only to be overruled.

And then I came across the Executive Summary of the Committee of Sponsoring Organizations of the Treadway Commission (COSO), which did not set out to use the poetic tool of assonance to amplify the definition of the boring subject of risk, but they left them in anyway:

"Risk is defined as the possibility that an event will occur *and adversely affect the achievement of objectives.*" [2]

And then later on in they moved from the letter 'a' to the letter 'e' in two separate sentences:

"Achieves *effective and efficient* operations when *external events* are considered ..."

145

and

> "... understands the extent to which operations are managed *effectively and efficiently* when *external events* may have ..."

This time, they managed to start four and then five words with an 'e', in this sentence about the impact internal controls can have on the attitude of management.

But what I liked best was the concept of 'tone at the top', which I found on page 4. It has a surprising ring to it, has it not? Especially when it relates to top management's attitude to internal control.

> "The board of directors and senior management establish tone at the top regarding the importance of internal control ..." [2] [3]

I admit that all this is a little meagre in a 10-page Executive Summary, but someone wrote it, someone reviewed it, and someone decided to leave these minor deviations in the report. And they do add a little fun, otherwise absent in the serious subject of internal control.

[1] IAS 37 – Provisions, Contingent Liabilities and Contingent Assets issued by the International Accounting Standards Board in 1998.

[2] Internal Control – Integrated Framework, Executive Summary, May 2013 issued by the Committee of Sponsoring Organizations of the Treadway Commission (COSO).

[3] As an aside, the FRC use the same word 'tone' in this context in their report 'Guidance on Risk Management, Internal Control and Related Financial and Business Reporting', September 2014, but they keep the tone serious, without using poetic diversion: 'The board should establish the tone for risk management and internal control ...', page 6.

ANNUAL REPORTS
Two ENTs

A subsequent event is exactly that: an event that happens after the preparation of the financial statements. But the two accounting boards say they don't start at the same time. This event is so important that accountants have had to invent rules to deal with it. As usual, the rule is not the same under IASB or FASB. What a surprise!

The IASB, in IAS 10, decrees that the 'subsequent' starts when the financial statements are 'authorised for issue', whereas the FASB (ASC 855) decrees the date is when the financial statements are issued. Not authorised for issue.

The two international accounting standard boards can't agree on a two-week window. They had the chance to keep the same date, but they decided, perhaps for accounting clarity, that different dates would be more relevant, or to show their independence from one another. But what is this window of difference?

Let's make a theoretical timetable of filing financial statements:

31st December	Year end
28th February	Financial statements completed
18th March	**The board of directors approve the financial statements (IASB in IAS 10)**
19th March	Announcement of financial results
1st April	**Financial statements made available to shareholders (FASB in ASC 855)**
15th May	Shareholders approve the financial statements
17th May	Financial statements filed

So we have this delay of approximately two weeks, which depends on the time it takes directors to issue the financial statements after approval. Two weeks is a short time, insignificant, but the two boards make it significant by disagreeing on the dates. I can give you no reason for this accounting confusion.

Who, then, is the culprit? IAS 10 was issued in April 2001, and ASC 855 in May 2009. Thus, the FASB knew and decided on a different date. What is also interesting is that the FASB only apply this rule to quoted US companies. For private US companies, they decided on the same date as the IASB. But of course they use different words: they talk about when the financial statements are 'available to be issued'. This clearly means when the directors have approved them. The time between approval and being available for issue is so small in private companies as to be irrelevant. Different words but the same meaning.

Is this another example of accountants being complicated? Explained like this, it makes them look ridiculous. But it does give them more work to do. If, for instance, a major client goes bankrupt or a major factory burns down on 25th March in the above timetable, the financial statements stay as they are under IASB rules, with any losses included in the next year's financial statements. However, under FASB, these losses must be included in the current year's financial statements.

I find it comical that the two boards can agree on this important concept, but spoil it with disagreement on the date to apply it, especially when the difference in timing is so insignificant.

Lament the insignificent.

Feet on the counter

How can it be that pharmaceutical companies cannot agree on the illegal trade in counterfeit drugs?

The World Health Organization estimates that falsified products account for 10% of the pharmaceutical market worldwide, rising to 30% in some countries. All therapeutic areas are affected, including vaccines. However, in markets where powerful regulatory controls are in place, falsified drugs are estimated to represent less than 1% of market value.

So I decided to compare how the eight pharmaceutical companies react in their risk statements and to see what they do about it.

Three of them worry about how illegal and counterfeit drugs could hurt their reputations: Bristol Myers Squibb, Johnson & Johnson, and Novartis. This leads them to conclude that their financial results could be affected and patients possibly harmed.

Two of them worry less. AstraZeneca only worries about future earnings related to the 'illegal trade' in their medicines, without noting any concern for their reputation or for their patients. Sanofi merely states that 'pharmaceutical companies face illegal competition from falsified drugs' and then moves on without indicating worries about financial results or reputation. However, Sanofi does worry about its reputation, not from counterfeit drugs, but from legal claims, product liability, data security breaches and social media.

Three companies do not worry and mention nothing in their annual reports. They opt for silence: Abbott Laboratories, AbbVie, and GSK. Have they discovered a secret elixir to immunise their drugs against the perils of counterfeiters, and refuse to reveal it?

They relax with their feet on the counter against the risk of counterfeit (counterfeet) drugs, instead of worrying about them.

Odd peculiar risks in financial reports

Some companies become surprisingly inventive with their business risks in annual reports. The risks I identify here are not material risks, but odd peculiar ones, which surprised me. Perhaps the risk statement was given to junior staff to write without any review, or perhaps someone made a mistake. Whatever the reason, I found a few to share with you.

Water stress risk

At first, I thought that GSK must have their factories in the desert because they cite water as a risk. But their factories are not in the desert. The issue lies in the fresh water they use in their manufacturing process. Their risk comes from the increase in levels of water stress giving their operations less water. [1]

They then go on to develop concepts such as 'water stewardship' and being 'water neutral', throwing in jargon such as a BAU [2] climate scenario and a TCFD [3] to make the risk difficult to understand. Finally, they announce that their water stress has a low risk level, with a low potential profit impact but with a long time frame of up to 10 years.

The reader is left questioning whether this risk is real. If they judge water stress a risk in countries where it is abundant, they should include earthquakes as a worldwide risk, which of course they don't. And then, they put in a risk of 'extreme weather', essentially flooding; this time too much water. Perhaps they should decide: too little or too much, but I am being facetious. If the company considers them material, they cannot conclude a 'low risk level'. If the company believes the risks are low, why put them in the report? They are neither logical nor consistent; I guess they must be more interested in following the climate trend.

Associated British Foods are a little more optimistic. They 'recognise water as a valuable shared resource that can be scarce in some parts of the world'. Water for them is not a risk, but a responsibility where they show the world how well they recycle their water, for instance:

> "Of the total water abstracted, 25% was reused within our operations before finally returning it to the watercourse."

Please go to page 73 of the 2021 annual report of Associated British Foods to witness the clarity of their prose with 'abstracted'. Is this the right word? I ask myself. An engineer might extract water. I would pump it or collect it or turn on the tap. If it is the right word, my apologies for being so lost in thought and preoccupied. They abstract water again on page 79, so it must be me.

I digress, back to the water risk. These companies use fashionable marketing to claim that they are 'climate considerate' and present us with their 'proof'. Either that, or they are confident that no-one will read this part of their report.

[1] GSK Annual Report 2021 page 50, under the heading Summary of GSK's risks and opportunities.

[2] BAU: business-as-usual (but with the hyphens).

[3] TCFD: Task Force on Climate-related Financial Disclosures (should really be TFCRFD; they missed an F and an R to confuse. But then, TFCRFD would be rather cumbersome).

Social media risk

Bristol Myers Squibb are pioneers. In their 2021 annual report 10-K, they introduce a new risk:

> "Increased use of social media platforms present risks and challenges."

(Grammatically, it should be either 'Increased **uses** of social media platforms **present** risks and challenges' or 'Increased **use** of social media platforms **presents** risks and challenges'. Not the one they have written, but I guess everyone understands anyway.)

They are afraid of inappropriate use of certain media vehicles and of 'inaccurate posts or comments.' All this, according to them, could damage their 'reputation, brand image and goodwill'.

Sanofi follow them as fellow pioneers. Their management are scared of this new technology, especially false information and inaccurate or inappropriate posts. They conclude that social media could have an adverse effect on their reputation, business, and financial results.

I guess other companies will follow this trend later, and social media will become a fashionable risk for all.

New or unknown risks

Let's agree that a risk is something bad that may happen in the future: the possibility of a loss in the accounting world. I have put the full definition from the *Oxford English Dictionary* below. [1] Some companies admit that they don't know what risks may strike – for instance, a meteor hitting their headquarters at 2am one morning. They call them new or unknown risks. But, and this is the thing, they believe they are so important that they must include them in their annual reports. An optimist might think these companies are trying to tell us they are on the lookout for these new risks. They pay a guard with binoculars on the roof 24 hours a day to seek out the meteor! I must be a pessimist, because I think an unknown risk is not a risk at all.

AstraZeneca go poetic and call them 'emerging'. They are in this fog and see a figure emerging. It must be a risk, so let's report it. They describe them as follows:

"Emerging risks are 'new' risks that **may** challenge us in the future."

The important word here is 'may'. But how can they be important, even material enough to put in a financial report, when they don't know what they are? But they make it more bizarre when they go on to say that they probably won't impact the business next year, they stay uncertain and may evolve rapidly and they may not happen at all. Unlikely, uncertain, may not materialise. They are imaginary. The heading should be called 'imaginary risks' and not emerging ones.

And finally they resort to gobbledygook when they announce that they scan the horizon with their SET function looking for these emerging risks with 'external insights'. SET is explained on page 4 of the report: Senior Executive Team. What could external insight be? Anyway, the two of them (the SET function and the external insights) meet and 'scan the horizon' to look for these emerging risks.

One should not take this metaphor of horizon scanning too literally. The Senior Executive Team does not stand on the beach looking out to sea, even after a few drinks at their seaside conference hotel. Apparently, horizon scanning refers to a methodology of future studies. They go on, but I will stop here. They complicate it so much that they become incomprehensible.

Johnson & Johnson have a similar worry with unknown risks and uncertainties that could adversely affect their results or their financial condition. They specify that it is not possible to predict or identify all risks. Everybody knows that! This is so evident, but perhaps companies need to remind their shareholders. The sun sets in the west on the horizon they scrutinise. Ice is cold. Fire is hot.

[1] *Oxford English Dictionary*, Risk: (Exposure to) the possibility of loss, injury, or other adverse or unwelcome circumstance; a chance or situation involving such a possibility.

Dividend risk

Most people believe companies that pay dividends revel in financial health. Why then put fear into the hearts of shareholders with risk statements such as this?

> "There can be no guarantee that we will pay dividends or repurchase stock."

Every normal shareholder knows that the board of directors decides the level of dividends, and that change has a positive or negative effect on the stock. Yet, instead of stating this in a neutral manner somewhere in their annual reports, they decide to call it a material risk and keep all aspects negative.

Some companies pay dividends, but have no dividend risk: Johnson & Johnson, AstraZeneca, GSK, Sanofi, and Novartis. AbbVie and Bristol Myers Squibb have a dividend risk.

As usual, there is no explication for these different approaches, but above all none on why these companies think a dividend is a material risk.

Delaware risk

Some US companies classify Delaware as a material risk. Delaware is a state of one million people on the east coast of the USA, whose capital is Dover in the county of Kent. Naturally, the state itself does not seem to present the risk, but its laws do. Company by-laws combined with Delaware law make life difficult for shareholders and can prevent changes to members of the board, delay takeovers and limit certain forms of lawsuits. But this is such an advantage for companies – it protects their boards from interference from obstreperous shareholders and outside influence – that Delaware has become a haven for registration of companies in the USA.

These companies do not mention why they choose Delaware as their place of incorporation. But these restrictions and difficulties are not simply perceived, they are real and protect directors in the company. How ironic, then, that directors transform this advantage into a material risk, which they highlight in their annual reports. Also, Delaware isn't famous for much else and doesn't try to be; they even boast about it, and other states are trying to copy them to get the business.

In parallel, other companies also incorporated in Delaware do not declare a Delaware-related risk. Amazon, for instance, is incorporated in Delaware, but declares no related risk.

Further, the risks are not the same. How odd is that? Bristol Myers Squibb have a long paragraph blaming the Court of Chancery of the State of Delaware for the restrictions they impose on legal claims against shareholders. These 'just what they want' provisions have become risks. AbbVie concentrate more on coercive takeover practices and inadequate takeover bids. But they do list restrictions on directors and stockholders.

These risks paragraphs show how useless risk statements are.

The irony of development

Development expenses under IFRS rules must be capitalised, whereas these same development expenses in the USA under FASB standards must be expensed. Yet ironically pharmaceutical companies under IFRS standards ignore the IFRS rule, treating development expenses in the same way as in the USA.

I compared the treatment of development expenses in the eight pharmaceutical companies I selected.

US companies start their section of accounting policies with a clear statement such as this one:

> "Research and development expenses are expensed as incurred."

European companies usually have something like this:

> "Research expenditure is charged to profit and loss in the year in which it is incurred."

The word 'development' is missing. They go on to explain that they capitalise development expenses when the six criteria of IAS 38 Intangible Assets are met. Sanofi are the most emphatic, adding the phrase 'if and only if' to show their studious application of the standard, and they list in detail the six criteria they follow, perhaps to convince the reader of their diligence.

But then the European companies put in their disclaimer which ensures the treatment of development expenses is similar in practice to FASB standard ASC 730, Research and Development, where they state that intangible assets cannot be capitalised until they have obtained marketing approval by the regulatory authorities.

So nothing is capitalised until the regulatory authorities officially approve the medicine or medical device. But the company cannot incur development expenses after regulatory approval, that is, when the product is complete and clinical trials have shown the benefits.

Expenses thereafter are marketing expenses, which companies cannot categorise as development expenses.

The Roche Group, in the above disclaimer, is categorical, whereas the others are more flexible when they add the words 'usually' not met (Sanofi and GSK) or 'almost invariably' (AstraZeneca). So sometimes, they capitalise development expenses, but they don't tell us when. AstraZeneca, though, do state that no capitalisation of development expenses has been included in their financial statements. Their 'almost invariably' means not capitalised, but they might capitalise in future years. Beware!

I will not speculate on whether the pharmaceutical companies consulted with each other to treat development costs in the same way, or whether the European companies think capitalisation of development expenses is ridiculous, or whether they are sending a subliminal message to the IASB:

> "Cancel the capitalisation of development expenses. This is an easy decision."

If it is subliminal, the IASB are not listening.

Matter to emphasise

When I first read the expression 'emphasis of matter', I thought it related to physics: something visible, heavy and interesting. But in accounting, this matter is invisible, ephemeral and part of an auditor's report. This matter, however, is important for an auditor, even if it is a devious matter.

It is a subject included in the financial statements that needs to be emphasised to the user of these same financial statements in the audit report. Thus, the expression they have invented is 'Emphasis of Matter'. This subject has to be of such importance that it is fundamental to understanding the financial statements. [1]

To help auditors, the IAASB give an example in their handbook:

> "Emphasis of Matter
> We draw attention to Note X of the financial statements, which describes the effects of a fire in the Company's production facilities.

Our opinion is not modified in respect of this matter." [2]

So a fire can be classified as Emphasis of Matter. This is a start, but one example is not enough. So I searched real auditors' reports to see what I could find. I read 30 audit reports from quoted companies in Europe, the USA and the UK, for the years 2021 and 2022, and I found no Emphasis of Matter paragraphs. This paragraph is rare in auditors' reports. But why?

The logical answer could simply be that the financial statements of these companies are so clear, that the auditor does not need to highlight any more information. Another auditor might give the official answer by quoting paragraph A6 on page 562 of the *Handbook*:

> "However, a widespread use of Emphasis of Matter paragraphs may diminish the effectiveness of the auditor's communication about such matters."

Why not use it often if the objective is only to help the 'understanding of the financial statements'? It would be so much easier to go directly to the auditor's report to find these fundamental matters, instead of reading the whole annual report to find them oneself.

In practice, however, Emphasis of Matter is NOT used to help the understanding of the financial statements. It is used to express the auditors' **worry** about the financial statements.

Auditors worry about the subject they choose to put in this paragraph. They're not so worried as to qualify their audit report, but worried enough to imply to users without stating their worry:

> "Beware! This is a serious problem in the company and you should worry about it too. I have done all the necessary work to give my opinion, but the company is now fragile from these matters."

I then went in search of audit reports that included a paragraph of Emphasis of Matter. They are not difficult to find because they are a sign of fragility often highlighted by the press, as a warning from the company's auditors. Here is a rather tame comment from an article in *The Times*:

"Cineworld's financial woes are outlined in yesterday's auditor's report. The group's statutory accounts were unqualified although they included an 'emphasis of matter in respect of material uncertainty around going concern'. One scenario paints a picture that would see covenants breached and the group unable to repay its $462.5 million revolving credit facility or continue as a going concern." [3]

This is a more emphatic one from *The Economist* in 2009:

"Bankers and regulators are haggling now with auditors about how to present their accounts. An auditor worried about whether a bank will be a going concern in 12 months' time may feel bound to write a cautioning paragraph, known as an 'emphasis of matter'. This could shake the public's already low faith in banks." [4]

The press show the worry, but auditors stay factual and official, as in the example above. They start Emphasis of Matter paragraphs with phrases such as:

"We draw attention to Note 2.1 to the financial statements."

They follow with 'if' and 'may' words, telling us that if this happens then something else may happen. And they finish off giving us reassurance with 'our opinion is not modified by this matter'.

Emphasis of Matter paragraphs, then, have nothing to do with understanding financial statements. Auditors use them as a warning of the financial health of the company, but without telling us. Devious, no?

[1] Here is the definition. Emphasis of Matter paragraph: 'A paragraph included in the auditor's report that refers to a matter appropriately presented or disclosed in the financial statements that, in the auditor's judgment, is of such **importance that it is fundamental to users' understanding** of the financial statements.' IAASB, *Handbook of International Quality Control, Auditing, Review, Other Assurance, and Related Services Pronouncements*, 2021 Edition Volume 1, page 15.

[2] International Auditing and Assurance Standards Board, IAASB, *Handbook of International Quality Control, Auditing, Review, Other Assurance, and Related Services Pronouncements*, 2021 Edition Volume 1, page 568.

[3] *The Times*, Cineworld keeping faith in recovery despite legal woes, 18th March 2022, by Dominic Walsh, https://www.thetimes.co.uk/article/cineworld-keeping-faith-in-recovery-despite-legal-woes-mtmgw57c8.

[4] *The Economist*, A gallant effort, January 15th 2009, https://www.economist.com/britain/2009/01/15/a-gallant-effort.

BBB

"Lord Agnew: Board of British Business Bank 'should be sacked' over Covid loans".

The Times published an article on 16th March 2022 with this headline. I thought I would check what happened to the members of the board thereafter, from their annual reports.

The bank has a new Chief Executive Officer and Chief Financial Officer. In addition, four other directors departed. No reasons were given. I have no idea whether these changes are related to Lord Agnew's comments.

The directors of the bank significantly disagree with Lord Agnew, who claimed 'a whole chain of weakness' in the management and oversight of the bounce back loan (BBL) scheme and resigned as a minister because of it. The bank makes two statements about the scheme in their 2023 annual report. Here they are:

> "The Board has assessed that the Bank has met its KPI on Covid Administration Lender Assurance with improved audit outcomes in re-audited delivery partners and has met its KPI relating to investigating fraud risk in Bounce Back Loan Scheme guarantee claims."

> "The Bounce Back Loan Scheme portfolio is currently performing above expectations, with anticipated credit loss levels lower than earlier estimates."

So, no problem. The directors have pushed Lord Agnew and his news under the carpet, or resolved the issues or ignored them for publication in their annual report. It is up to the readers to decide.

But the article gave me the idea of reading the rest of the annual report of the British Business Bank, now known as the BBB. Do not confuse BBB with the BBL, the Bounce Back Loan Scheme, because the BBB manages the BBL.

There are six BBs in the annual report. Two we already know, the BBB and the BBL, but another two simple ones exist: the BBI (British Business Investments, sometimes referred to as British Business Investments Limited and not BBIL to confuse us, no doubt) and the BBF (British Business Finance). Note that 'Bank' has been dropped from these abbreviations. But there are two more complicated BBs: the BBFL (British Business Finance Limited) and the BBFSL (British Business Financial Services Ltd).

So there you go! BBs are popular.

I enjoy reading annual reports published by government organisations because they congratulate themselves for their great work and promote their organisation as ideal, in direct opposition to Lord Agnew. The British Business Bank is no exception. 'An Extraordinary Year' is the title of the Chair's statement, with no mention of the loss incurred or the problems with Covid. 'A Renewed Focus on Growth' is the title of the Chief Executive's statement. I would hope so after a drop in gross operating income and a 'fall in valuations' across their equity portfolio. As expected, the Financial Officer's report is more factually moderate with his title, 'Our financial performance in context'.

But I was overwhelmed by the good deeds of the bank described on pages 20 and 21. They benefit business, support business, unlock potential, provide vast amounts of information to the 547k visitors to the website, and deliver over 100,000 start-up loans, all this in the 'UK economy facing significant headwinds'.

So, no worries: the BBB is on track, despite the headwinds, the losses, the fall in valuations, the chain of weaknesses and the resignations.

MAGAZINE ARTICLES
Superior British accountants

"BRITISH accountants have always considered themselves superior to their fellows in America."

This surprising statement does not come from me. I don't have the knowledge or expertise to make such a claim. In any case, where on earth do you find evidence to prove it? Even if it is true, I would not have the courage to proclaim it. The ire of my fellow accountants in both countries would be so great, it would force me into hiding.

It was written in *The Economist* in 2002. [1]

The article goes on to claim that 'the Brits tend to come with better grades and from better universities', which is again an incredible claim, but their conclusion is even more staggering:

"This means, naturally, that they (the Brits) are possessed of more strength of character and backbone when facing finance directors intent on cooking the books."

Okay, so this statement is over 20 years old and cannot be relevant today! American universities have had the time to come up to the standards of the British. Their grades will have surely improved or perhaps the British ones have slumped somewhat. The combined strength of character and backbone of we British accountants, I claim, is intact. And anyway, there are so few finance directors intent on cooking anything, especially books, on the eastern side of the Atlantic.

Has anything changed in the situation since 2002? What are the qualifications of finance directors in the two countries today?

Below are two statements, one from the *Wall Street Journal* in 2020 to describe the situation in the USA. Mark Maurer writes:

"At the 1,000 largest US public companies, the portion of CFOs who are certified public accountants fell to about 36% last year, according to data from organizational consulting firm Korn Ferry."
[2]

The other was written by Chrissy Chui on the site The CFO in 2018 to describe the situation in Britain. She writes:

> "In fact, skills in accountancy and finance are a near requisite for regional and FTSE companies – two thirds of FTSE 100 CFOs come from the Big Four auditors KPMG, Deloitte, EY [Ernst & Young] and PwC [PricewaterhouseCoopers]." [3]

So in the USA, CFOs do not need to be professional accountants, and only 36% are, whereas in Britain that figure is 66.6%. Not only that, but they have also worked for the Big Four, not with just any old accounting firm – the assumption being, of course, that working for the Big Four is 'better' than working for anyone else. I guess only people who have worked both inside and outside the Big Four can judge. [4]

Now, let's make a rather spectacular assumption: after 20 years, British accountants no longer consider themselves superior to their fellows in America, and that universities and grades are now at the same level in the two countries. Let's also assume that there is no difference in the strength of character and backbone of American and British accountants.

Even with these assumptions, nothing changes from the conclusions of the original article in *The Economist*. Approximately 60% of US CFOs are not accountants in the large quoted companies, whereas only 30% are not accountants in Britain. This surely means, to quote *The Economist* again, that

> "… naturally, they (the Brits) are possessed of more strength of character and backbone when facing finance directors intent on cooking the books"

simply because there are more professionally qualified accountants in these positions in Britain than in America, and, of course, professional accountants have more strength of character and backbone than non-accountants. No further discussion possible here! QED!

[1] *The Economist*, 13th July 2002, Section – Finance & Economics, 'Auditing It could happen here.'

[2] *The Wall Street Journal*, 29th January 2020, CFO JOURNAL, 'Why You Don't Need to Be an Accountant to Be a CFO,' by Mark Maurer.

[3] The qualifications and qualities that CFOs and FDs must possess to get to the top, 9th October 2018, by Chrissy Chui, https://the-cfo.io/

[4] I have had the privilege of working for both: one of the Big Four and a small accounting practice of 20 people, where I spent five years in articles. But I refuse to judge.

To ding not dong financial results

I didn't know it was possible to 'ding' financial results until I read the *Wall Street Journal*:

> "Companies use LIFO to lower their taxable income. But to do so, they also must use it for financial accounting, even though it can ding financial results." [1]

This sentence is music to my ears. Although I'm not sure what ding means in a financial context, I can only imagine that the results are so impressive that they're creating a symphony of congratulations for the company's directors. Surely the meaning of ding, here, is not the now obsolete sense of pompous or arrogant financial statements, which would render the sentence unintelligible.

But, given the Scottish origins of this word – to batter the enemy or to ding them to death – I suspect the financial results of this particular company slumped because of their last in, first out (LIFO) inventory valuation.

I find dinged (or is it dung?) so much more entertaining than the mundane 'reduced' or 'fallen' used by us accountants to describe poor financial results.

[1] *Wall Street Journal*, CFO Journal, Inflation Puts Spotlight on Companies' Use of Last-In, First-Out Accounting, by Kristin Broughton, 27th June 2022.

FORMAL REPORTS
Professional scepticism or deep suspicion

Auditors must carry out audits using professional scepticism, with a 'k'. [1] What can this be? I know what scepticism means when associated with religion, but not with a business. The IAASB have a handbook [2] to explain it to us, so I had a look.

First it tells us why professional scepticism is necessary. This part I skipped through quickly, but I found this surprising statement: professional scepticism is an attitude. Not a doubt, but an attitude:

> "Professional skepticism [1] is an attitude that is applied by the auditor when making professional judgments …"

As an auditor, I never had to turn on an attitude to make an audit judgement, and then turn it off to check the accounts. I simply checked what management prepared in their financial accounts.

But what if you don't have professional scepticism or know how to turn it on? Is it the same, for instance, as a 'will to win'? I can turn off my will to win when I play football in the garden with the grandchildren. But if I don't have it in the first place, can I ever turn it on? I digress.

How to apply professional scepticism

The *Handbook* goes on to explain how auditors should apply scepticism, with a list of events and actions to take. For example, if directors give contrary information, auditors turn on professional scepticism and move into action by questioning, considering and being alert. However, the list is not all-inclusive and is, anyway, optional. Auditors can do whatever they want by using their professional judgement. And then comes the surprise: auditors should record their instances of professional scepticism – not to show how excellently they audit, but more to 'provide evidence' of their 'exercise of professional skepticism'.

They should record scepticism when they come across management contradictions, in comparing management estimates with their own, and when they carry out additional audit procedures in instances of contradiction or management bias.

Scepticism Chart

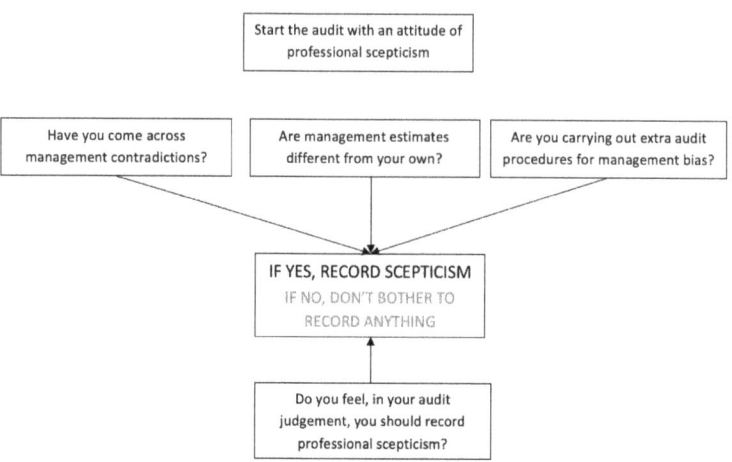

The IAASB do not teach professional scepticism. They simply tell auditors why it is important and when to apply it. I guess no-one can teach it. You either have it naturally or you acquire it through experience, but only then can you understand this section in the *Handbook*.

Suspicious mindset
Scepticism though is not enough, so the IAASB launched a discussion paper in January 2021 to see whether auditors should have a more aggressive attitude, asking the question:

> "Would requiring a 'suspicious mindset' contribute to enhanced fraud identification when planning and performing the audit? Why or why not?"

A certain Lord Brydon wrote a report in which he recommends a 'mindset of deep suspicion in relevant circumstances, rather than just scepticism'. [3] Auditors should go back and forth between professional scepticism and a suspicious mindset. I can imagine them in a conversation with the directors of the company, where they switch between the two, depending on the relevant circumstances. Quite a programme! And what a performance in mental gymnastics.

It would be easier to choose the attitude by the day of the week such as this:

Monday	Professional scepticism day
Tuesday	Day off
Wednesday	Professional scepticism day
Thursday	Day off
Friday	Deep suspicion day

PricewaterhouseCoopers disagree with having an attitude of suspicion, and they do it with eloquence, by emphasising a change of temperature in the workplace:

> Deep suspicion 'could also have the unintended consequence of potentially chilling important dialogue with management …' [4]

The National Association of State Boards of Accountancy in the USA take a more verbose administrative tone to disagree. They are afraid that the auditor–client relationship would be damaged by the 'adversarial connotation' of a suspicious mindset. [5]

Chilling dialogue is more vivid than adversarial connotation, is it not? Accepting both the chilling and adversarial, the IAASB kept professional scepticism instead of suspicious mindset.

---

[1] I use UK English spelling and style overall, except when quoting from text written in US English. For instance, the IAASB in their *Handbook* use US English, thus 'skepticism', when I stray from UK English, just twice.

[2] International Auditing and Assurance Standards Board, IAASB, *Handbook of International Quality Control, Auditing, Review, Other Assurance, and Related Services Pronouncements*, 2021 Edition, Volume 1.

[3] Sir Donald Brydon led an independent review at the invitation of government, to consider how the audit process could better serve the needs of users and the wider public interest: https://assets.publishing.service.gov.uk/media/5df8edfced915d0938597e1f/brydon-review-final-report.pdf.

[4] Letter dated 29th January 2021 to Mr Willie Botha, Technical Director,

International Auditing and Assurance Standards Board, signed by James Chalmers on behalf of the network of member firms of PricewaterhouseCoopers International Limited.

[5] Letter dated 19th January 2021 to the International Auditing and Assurance Standards Board, A. Carlos Barrera CPA, NASBA Chair, and Ken L. Bishop, NASBA President and CEO.

Chapter 5

Bemused

JARGON
The ghosts of the tax gap

I know of an accounting GAAP; now I learn of a tax gap. And the HRMC are proud of theirs. I quote:

> "HMRC is the only tax authority in the world that measures and publishes tax gap estimates annually in such a comprehensive way." [1]

This is now the fourth gap I think of when I step off the London Underground. It must be important, so here is their definition:

> "The tax gap is the difference between the amount of tax that should, in theory, be paid to HMRC and what is actually collected." [2]

I must appear ignorant, but this is the first time I have ever read the HMRC annual report. [1] I am, after all, a mere member of the ICAEW and not one from the Chartered Institute of Public Finance and Accountancy (CIPFA). HMRC publish an annual tax gap report, [3] so they give us the detail and an amount, £35.8 billion. Using my simple chartered accountant approach and still ignorant of the tax gap, I think this means that HMRC has not collected and will not collect £35.8 billion of taxes during the year. They are proud of the amount they have collected: 95.2% of all tax due.

And so by omission, they are proud of the amount they missed, £35.8 billion. My opinion differs from theirs. This is a massive amount of missed opportunity. So I had a look into how they calculate it.

I suppose a large part of this tax gap comes from criminals, especially illegal drugs and unrecorded cash transactions from what is also called the shadow economy, subterranean economy or underground economy. But this is not what they have calculated in Figure 1.4 Tax gap by customer group – share of tax gap.

"The tax gap from small businesses is the largest proportion of the tax gap by customer group, at 56%." [3]

And criminals only have about 11%. Now that is surprising. In other words, £20 billion of taxes should be paid by small businesses and are not. HMRC know about them but don't collect the taxes. But, as I said, I am not an expert on the tax gap.

I then had a look at who the criminals are in their tax gap analysis. In 'Table 1.1: Tax gap components 2021 to 2022 estimates' the hidden economy only contributes £1.4 billion to the tax gap of £35.8 billion, made up of ghosts and moonlighters who do not pay their income tax and capital gains tax. I then searched for the definition of ghosts and moonlighters. A ghost is someone whose total income is unknown to HMRC and a moonlighter is someone whose income is partially unknown to HMRC.

That was another surprise for me, not so much the amount, but the names HMRC gives the members of the hidden economy: ghosts and moonlighters. And now I repeat myself, I am not an expert on the tax gap.

[1] His Majesty's Revenue and Customs, HMRC, Annual Report and Accounts, 2022 to 2023, page 17.

[2] His Majesty's Revenue and Customs, HMRC, Annual Report and Accounts, 2022 to 2023, page 200.

[3] The latest tax gap report can be found at www.gov.uk/government/collections/measuring-tax-gaps.

Pretentious jargon

Accountants have an unusual way of constructing jargon in standard costing. They take common words, mostly nouns, string them together, call it an accounting term, and then use the initials. Their simplest variance is called Direct Material Cost Variance or DMCV.

The first word, 'direct', is superfluous here because indirect is meaningless in this context. 'Material' brings connotations of textile fabric or importance as in 'material difference'. Neither of these applies. Nor does the abstract, 'he's certainly college material'. Nor does it mean material as in important as in the phrase 'in all material respects' used by auditors, which I have already written about. Material here is the product being made in the factory. Only an accountant could guess that. Finally, 'cost' is not cost, but as I will show later has up to five components.

The DMCV is the difference between the cost and the standard, a simple subtraction. But accountants prefer to have not one result (too easy) but three. And then they give the three variances five names: price variance, usage variance, yield, mix variance and sub-usage variance. For example, they call the last one Material Sub-usage Variance. Why five names when three would do? Their explanations and justifications cover whole chapters in textbooks.

One of their simpler explanations is that 'sometimes the usage variance equals the yield variance, but not always'. The 'not always' here requires accounting students to learn another obscure concept called RSQ, revised standard quantity, which gives this marvellous formula:

$$\text{Direct Material Cost Variance, DMCV} = \{(\textbf{RSQ}\text{-AQ}) \times \text{SP}\} + \{(\text{SQ-}\textbf{RSQ}) \times \text{SP}\} + \{\text{AQ} \times (\text{SP-AP})\}$$

If this is not confusing, then nothing is! Mix and yield variances need a chapter on their own. And how banal and vague to choose sub-usage as an official accounting term!

This, you might think, is complicated, but if I now move to their most sophisticated variance, the Overhead Variance, they confuse us even more.

To remain unintelligible, accountants invent not one but two Overhead Variances: variable and fixed. Why two, you might ask? Management wonders too, because generally they don't know the difference between the two. One of the variances becomes the bizarre 'variable variance', the Variable Overhead Variance or VOV.

VOV, as you might know, is an Italian egg liqueur invented by Gian Battista Pezziol, in 1845, well before the accounting profession took it up as an accounting term. Maybe accountants had a little too much of it when they were looking for a new accounting term, or they liked it so much, they called a variance after it, without letting us know.

Accountants then explain the four variances that make up the Fixed Overhead Variance: Fixed Overhead **Expenditure** Variance, Fixed Overhead **Efficiency** Variance, Fixed Overhead **Volume** Variance and Fixed Overhead **Capacity** Variance. You can see they use their unusual jargon technique by stringing four words together – I suppose, in their eyes, to make it consistent.

This quote by David Ogilvy, the late British advertising tycoon and founder of Ogilvy & Mather, must apply to some members of the accounting profession:

> "Our business is infested with idiots who try to impress by using pretentious jargon." [1]

[1] Quotation attributed to David Ogilvy by azquotes.com.

STANDARDS
When is an accounting principle an assumption?

You will remember that, in previous chapters, I wrote about the ten US accounting principles. However, to apply these principles, the American accounting profession decree, not too loudly, that accountants must understand accounting assumptions, [1] which come before these ten principles. But they are not sure whether there are three or four of them.

They have no doubt about the first three. The first assumption states that a business is separate from its owners. This seems obvious but let's give them merit for stating it. The second assumes that financial statements are prepared with dollar amounts. I'm not sure what other currency Americans would insist on. Or that accountants must prepare the statements with one currency. Why on earth would they mix currencies except to fool the reader? Again, let's give them credit for stating clearly the need to stick to one currency, the US dollar.

For the third, companies should prepare financial statements on an annual basis. Sometimes they call this the Time Period Assumption, in which case accounting transactions should be recorded within the year. Again, I'm sure no-one would accept a period of less or more than a year (except, of course, the 52- and 53-week year). Financial statements covering less than a year would be too time-consuming and those for more than a year, say every ten years, would be silly. In addition, what logical person would state that they record accounting transactions outside of the year in question? But let's again give them credit for stating it.

It is with the fourth accounting assumption that my doubts start to emerge. Not every accountant agrees it should be part of the assumptions. It states that a company continues to exist and does not go bankrupt. This assumption is the same as going concern, about which I have written extensively. Some accountants think this assumption is repetitive. They say that US GAAP have been emphasised and published so much that there is no need to have it as an accounting assumption as well.

It is odd how the accounting profession hides these assumptions, giving them such a low profile compared to US GAAP. Perhaps it is because they are not generally accepted, given the disagreement over the fourth assumption. In which case, they would have to call them US Accounting Assumptions, USAA. Most people would think this wouldn't work, but in the alphabet soup of the accounting world, USAA does not seem any more weird or unworkable than other sets of accounting letters.

For what it's worth, I recommend the use of USAA.

[1] *Accounting Theory*, by Alice Tuovila, 14th July 2019: https://www.coursehero.com/file/76653675/Accounting-Theorydocx/.

The mysterious user of financial statements

The IASB can't make up their mind who uses financial statements. They explain three users in IAS 1, from the specific to the general, without choosing the one we need to identify with.

I have already written about the first one, hidden in paragraph 7 as part of the definition of 'material', a place where no-one would search for it. This is the 'primary user'. Remember, primary users are existing and potential investors, lenders and other creditors. So this user, although primary, must be the one who defines material and does nothing else. If you have a question about the way a company sets its materiality limits, find a primary user and discuss it with them.

It should be noted that a primary user has a 'reasonable knowledge of business' and reviews and analyses the information diligently. I suppose this information relates to that information provided in the financial statements, even if that's not stated. However, the IAS does not give us any guidance about primary users who do not have a reasonable knowledge of the business. What if they don't have this reasonable knowledge, but are still users? We're left in an unsettling limbo.

The second user, according to paragraph 9, reads financial statements to make 'economic decisions' about the company in question. Now this user could still be the primary user above but is also a user who may not be an investor, lender or creditor. And they do not necessarily have reasonable knowledge of business as the primaries do. IAS 1 does not explain if this person might be a potential lender who decides not to lend. This person has probably read the financial statements and made an economic decision by deciding not to do anything.

The third and final user, according to paragraph 7, as part of the definition of general purpose financial statements, is not in a position to request information from the company. This describes anybody anywhere in the world. They read the general purpose financial statements and then sit back and do nothing, as I do.

A user cannot be all three of these at the same time. I am not sure what the IASB is trying to tell us. Have they done this on purpose? Did they make a mistake? Are they hoping nobody will discover the anomaly? Does it matter anyway? Whatever their intentions, they could at least make up their minds.

Are practical expedients practical?

Accounting standards generally set the rules and leave no room for deviation. However, the work involved in implementing the standards on leasing and revenue recognition for both the FASB and the IASB was so great that the two boards allowed exceptions intended to reduce the workload of implementation. As usual, instead of using a simple term – say, 'exception' or 'exceptions on implementation' – the two boards invented another more obscure one, 'practical expedients'. For once they agreed to use the same term. Examples of practical expedients are given in the standards, but there is no definition.

As a result, accountants cannot agree on exactly how to describe a practical expedient. Some define it as a relief effort, which is not helpful. Others call it an accounting policy election that provides relief, which is confusing. The explanation I like best is 'shortcut'. Perhaps they are all three: a relief effort shortcut. In any event, accounting literature seems to accept that a practical expedient should make it simpler for companies to comply with the standards.

But they don't always succeed, because once a practical expedient is chosen, it must be used thereafter, as explained in paragraph 3 of IFRS 15 Revenue from Contracts with Customers:

> "An entity shall apply this Standard, including the use of any practical expedients, consistently to contracts with similar characteristics and in similar circumstances."

And it must be disclosed as stated in paragraph 129 of IFRS 15:

> "If an entity elects to use the practical expedient … the entity shall disclose that fact."

It seems that some companies elected to use a practical expedient, only to find it wasn't practical at all, and gave them more work than was initially estimated. They decided on the criteria of simplicity, time to implement and cost when choosing whether to elect for a practical expedient. But is this right? Should companies not choose, as the criteria, the noblest reason from the mission of both accounting boards, namely that of providing useful information to investors and other users of financial reports? And not merely mundane costs.

This made me think of this reflection from the late Alan Paton, the South African writer:

> "Ask yourself not if this or that is expedient, but if it is right." [2]

[1] International Financial Reporting Standards 15 Revenue from Contracts with Customers, IFRS 15, Paragraph 63.

[2] Quotation attributed to Alan Paton by azquotes.com.

'As if' mixed with 'even if'

Even if you are not an expert in IASB standards, read the definition below **as if** you were.

The most complicated IASB Standard, IFRS 9, regulates financial instruments. I will quote just one sentence, as an example, which might be easy to understand for a specialist in finance but is impossible for the mere accountant preparing financial statements.

Here it is:

> "A contract to buy or sell a nonfinancial item that can be settled net in cash or another financial instrument, or by exchanging financial instruments, as if the contract was a financial instrument, may be irrevocably designated as measured at fair value through profit or loss even if it was entered into for the purpose of the receipt or delivery of a nonfinancial item in accordance with the entity's expected purchase, sale or usage requirements."

The first line is encouraging because it is easy to understand, but then in the second line they throw in an 'as if', which is unsettling and encourages the reader to stop and read no further. But don't stop. Keep going, because they make it worse with the 'even if'. And then force you to read to the end, where you realise that you have understood nothing.

Difficult, isn't it? But don't try reading it a second time, it isn't worth the effort.

Now I am sure they meant well and wanted to include everything in their definition, but by doing so they managed to make it unintelligible.

Even if you don't understand it, read it **as if** you do.

Assets are invisible

Accounting standards declare that an asset is a right, not a right as in wrong or as in left, but as something due. Most of us, even the average accountant, believe that an asset is a physical object, a car or building, which we can see and touch. However, an asset, for the accountants who wrote the standards, is invisible because it is the right to own this car or that house.

Now, you probably don't believe me, so let's go to the official definitions in the accounting standards. The Conceptual Framework for Financial Reporting issued by the IASB states the definition of an asset in paragraph 4.3 as the following:

> "An asset is a present economic resource controlled by the entity as a result of past events."

Your first reaction will be that an asset is 'a present economic resource' and that this is not a right. But this reaction is incorrect because in the next paragraph the Conceptual Framework states that 'an economic resource is a right'. If you combine the two paragraphs in the Conceptual Framework, you understand more easily what they mean:

> "An asset is a right that has the potential to produce economic benefits and that is controlled by the entity as a result of past events."

Under US GAAP the definition of an asset is:

> "An asset is a present right of an entity to an economic benefit." [1]

So there we have it, accounting standard setters believe a physical asset is invisible, because it is a 'right'. And you can't see a right.

But the Conceptual Framework does admit in paragraph 4.12:

"Nevertheless, describing the set of rights as the physical object will often provide a faithful representation of those rights in the most concise and understandable way."

What a relief! Invisible they might be, but one is allowed to imagine the 'physical object' as described to represent this invisible right. This is what everyone does anyway!

And then hidden away in IAS 38, the IASB slip in another definition similar to the one in the Conceptual Framework. It stays a resource, but this time not an economic one. Here is the definition:

"An asset is a resource: (a) controlled by an entity as a result of past events; and (b) from which benefits are expected to flow to the entity." [2]

This resource is invisible too, so the board remains consistent, and they use similar terms, for instance, 'past events' and 'controlled by an entity'. BUT an asset as a right has disappeared without explanation. To stop any reflection, just as I am doing here, the board surprise us with a short note:

"The definition of an asset in this Standard was not revised, following the revision of the definition of an asset in the Conceptual Framework for Financial Reporting issued in 2018."

Again, no explanation of why; I conclude laziness.

[1] FASB Statement of Financial Accounting Concepts No. 8 Conceptual Framework for Financial Reporting, Chapter 4, Elements of Financial Statements, December 2021, Definition of Elements, Assets, E16.

[2] International Accounting Standard 38, Intangible Assets, IAS 38, paragraph 8.

ANNUAL REPORTS
Hide it in the balance sheet

I have already discussed development costs in relation to the pharmaceutical companies. Now I'll reveal what they do with both research and development costs. They announce they are expensed, but this is not always true.

Many have included capitalised research and development costs in their balance sheets, but they camouflage them by not highlighting where they are. The ordinary reader of financial statements must find this confusing, but only if they find them.

GSK, for instance, put them under the heading 'Licensed patents, amortised brands etc', which includes amounts 'still in development' without specifying a figure. AstraZeneca put them in 'Product, marketing and distribution rights', which is not the same. We know this because there is an important impairment charge, which they say is 'recorded against products in development'. Sanofi are more open because they have a clearer heading, 'Acquired R&D'. This gives us the clue. When companies purchase research and development, they capitalise them.

Roche Group even has a heading, 'Intangible assets not available for use'. I am not sure how they can have a value and be recorded without impairment. But they do give us some information: 'these assets mostly represent in-process research and development assets acquired', and then they explain the different types of acquisition.

American companies camouflage them elsewhere in the balance sheet. AbbVie, for instance, has 'indefinite-lived research and development' assets with a net carrying amount of K€1,877. Abbott and Johnson & Johnson also have 'intangible assets which relate to IPR&D [1] acquired in a business combination'. Note that the IP here does not refer to the more famous Internet Protocol, as in IP address, or the well-known Intellectual Property.

So, even when both the FASB and IASB standards have the same rules, the companies put them in the balance sheet in different places. European pharmaceutical companies tend to state their 'purchased R&D' in vague terms. The US companies use acronyms and odd peculiar accounting terms such as 'indefinite-lived' assuming that the normal user is educated enough in accounting terms to understand them.

Companies will claim they are not hiding anything. It's like putting shoes in the fridge. They will be found, but only when you open the door for a snack or read all the notes to the financial statements.

[1] Abbott and Johnson & Johnson do not reveal what IPR&D stands for: In-Process Research & Development. They assume that the ordinary user of financial statements knows what it means. Bristol Myers Squibb use 'IPRD', an acronym that is not quite the same, but similar, to keep the confusion alive.

Mostly 52, sometimes 53

Convention decrees that companies fix a period for their financial statements. The majority choose a year, at the end of a month. Any month. Only one organisation I know chooses a date that is not at the end of the month, the UK tax authorities, who decree that their year ends on 5th April.

Then there are the rebellious few that wish to stand out and be completely different. They choose 364 days as their year, or 'period' as they call it. I have often wondered why they think 364 days is better than 365. They must believe that this one day is important to leave out, but they never tell us why. The 364 is of course 52 weeks, and these companies maintain with force that this improves comparability. It does the opposite.

Sometimes the 52 weeks end on a Friday and sometimes a Saturday. Some companies even choose different months to end their 'period':

> "The Company's fiscal year ends on the Saturday nearest January 31."

So for this company, The Kroger Co., sometimes this Saturday is at the end of January and sometimes at the beginning of February.

The most surprising choice of year end comes from Associated British Foods, who chose the middle of September:

"The Group's consolidated financial statements are prepared to the Saturday nearest to 15 September. Accordingly, they have been prepared for the 53 weeks ended 18 September 2021."

I wonder what the historical reason for choosing the middle of a month could be: the founder's birthday, harvest time or the statement: 'Our company is different.'

But 364 days doesn't work all the time. Every once in a while, these companies decide to have a period of 371 days, seven days extra. How logical is that? But 'Ah!' their accountants will say, we do this to make sure that the 52 weeks finish more or less at the same time of the year. If this is their reasoning then why not use the 12-month model? We are back to my initial wondering.

In addition, comparisons year on year, or 52 weeks on 52 weeks, are lost, and now they use phrases such as:

"Group revenue was in line with last year on a reported basis."

All of a sudden, they ignore a year of 53 weeks with a previous year of 52. Revenues in reality declined by 2.2%, with no explanation. How convenient! The whole argument for 52-week reporting, that of better comparability from year to year, is quietly ignored.

But when it's convenient, instead of 'reporting basis', another expression is used, 'adjusted basis':

"On an adjusted basis profit before tax was up 49%."

And suddenly it makes more sense to use the percentage increase and bring both years to 52 weeks. Again, how convenient!

Fifty-two weeks also allows bizarre interim reporting. Most companies divide the 52 weeks by four and call it quarterly reporting. Others split the year into two unequal periods, one of 24 weeks and the other of 28, instead of two of 26 weeks. They don't call it half-yearly reporting of course, but interim reporting. And when one of the years is 53 weeks that messes up comparisons for at least one reporting period.

The only logical thing about 52-weeks reporting is that it brings reporting the closest one can get to a year, otherwise there is nothing logical about it, but accountants keep it because their mysterious history wins over logic, and they believe it makes them look better.

Really a risk?

This is my last moan about risks in annual reports. Pharmaceutical companies use ordinary parts of their business to pad out their risk statements, often using the excuse that management can mess things up, which constitutes a risk.

Sanofi, in their 2021 annual report, seem to agree with me because they are one of the few who admit the possibility of 'unsuccessful management' of a series of matters affecting their business, for instance the environment and governance. And then, as they all do, they use the standard phrase 'could adversely affect' with a list that follows: this time reputation and expectations of stakeholders.

Unsuccessful management of any business matters could result in the company experiencing difficulties, and could go as far as to put the company at risk of going bankrupt.

Competition

Take, for instance, competition. All companies without exception have competitors and all companies consider competition a major risk. The risk statements of the eight pharmaceutical companies I analysed all listed the competition as a risk.

Sanofi's is apparently the strongest with their fierce local competition, which is increasing. [1] GlaxoSmithKline choose to use the expression intense competition [2] as do Johnson & Johnson:

> "The Company's Consumer Health businesses face intense competition from other branded products and retailers' private-label brands." [3]

Now everybody knows that competition is fierce, intense and increasing. These bland statements do not help the reader understand what is going on. They describe business as usual. But they paint an alarming situation with the conclusion: the competition could adversely affect the business, results of operations or financial results.

And what are they going to do to combat this risk? After all, if it is so important that it needs to be included in the annual report, they cannot sit around and do nothing. They need to take action to combat this significant risk. It is here that the companies differ.

Some do stress-testing (GSK) and the risk diminishes to a mere possible increase in funding and, anyway, given the liquidity available they have nothing to worry about. Others do not make stress tests, but Hoffman La Roche (a pharmaceutical company not in my chosen eight) announce they might have to make more investments, so again there's nothing to worry about. This to me means the risk is minimal and should not be part of the risk analysis! Some perform supplementary 'management actions' (AstraZeneca) to combat the risks, but these are often meaningless actions such as 'diversified portfolio' or 'focus on key products'.

Some do nothing (Sanofi, Abbott). They state the risks and leave the reader to wonder whether they are real or imminent. The attitude appears to be this:

> "Every other company includes competition as a risk, so we will too."

Despite their stress-testing, GSK are gung-ho against their competition, as in this sentence:

> "Go beyond – this is about our hunger and desire, our drive to be better, to move with pace, and to outperform the competition."

With this hunger and desire, the competition has no chance! And yet GSK still announce that they have more intense competition, increased pricing pressure in both the US and Europe.

This is still business as usual. If companies stated they were losing market share in a particular region or segment, we would have information, but these bland but alarming competitive statements tell us nothing.

Manufacturing and international operations
Competition is not the only aspect of business as usual that can be presented as a risk. Many treat manufacturing as a risk. They have such complicated manufacturing processes that if 'interruptions or delays' were to occur, adverse effects would again appear. How obvious is that?

International operations are another. These companies choose to move into international markets, and then they classify their move as a risk. Working internationally is difficult, they say, because with so many international regulations and laws, they may not be able to keep up and may not see the changes that governments make.

Most of them make a formal statement similar to this one: 'The negative results of non-compliance with laws and regulations could adversely affect the business, the operating results and the financial condition of the company.'

If this risk is so major then get out, stay local and stop complaining.

Patient safety
A risk specific to the pharmaceutical industry concerns patient safety. However, governments worldwide have stepped in to control the industry. One could therefore argue that the risk moves from the pharmaceutical companies to the governments. If all parties follow the regulations, and if the regulations are adequate, the risk disappears. Unfortunately, multiple incidences of failure have resulted in patients suffering or dying after taking drugs, so all eight companies include patient safety as a risk, in some form or another.

Some concentrate on following regulations. For example, Abbott worry about the abundance of regulations coming from the US Food and Drug Administration (FDA) and other international regulatory agencies. [4]

Many companies complain about cost. Abbott again:

> "Compliance with these laws and regulations is costly and materially affects the business." [4]

A few go straight in and take the blame for patient safety, without hiding behind governments and their regulations. This is what GlaxoSmithKline write:

> "If we do not effectively manage risks to our patient safety activities, the most serious repercussion could be harm to patients." [5]

And, of course, harm to patients could also lead to severe damage to the reputation of the company, litigation, loss of trust among patients and healthcare providers, and loss of shareholder confidence.

Cyber security

There exists, however, a real risk which is also business as usual for every company, relating to information technology and cyber security. Companies today cannot survive without information technology and a focus on cyber security is essential to keep it running smoothly. But companies have leapt on this as a chance to spray buzzwords around to show how important it is and how seriously they are taking it. The list is long:

> "cyber attack, malicious intrusion, breakdown, destruction, loss of data privacy, target of malware, hacking, data leakage, invasion, corruption of data, security breaches, disruption, degradation or breakdown".

And then, when this is done, they state the inevitable 'BUT'. Despite all our efforts 'there can be no assurance that our measures and efforts will prevent future attacks' or something similar.

Having announced this risk, then what? Understandably, none of the companies give us information or assurance on the state of their defences. This would give information to hackers. They leave the risk hanging there for the investors and readers to worry about. But this gives us no more information than we knew before reading the risk statement. Everyone knows they are in a threatening cyber security environment, but this is just business as usual.

Summary

Risk statements in annual reports have become a list of 'I told you so's'. If ever there is a problem management can say: 'Well, we put this potential risk into our risk statement. We are competent managers doing an excellent job in a complex environment. Don't worry.'

[1] Sanofi, Form 20-F, Fiscal year ending 31st December 2021, page 5. It is interesting to note that the 'increasingly fierce local competition' becomes a mere 'increasingly local competition'. Fierce has disappeared, so, I assume, competition is less international, more local. Difficult to imagine.

[2] GlaxoSmithKline, annual report, fiscal year ending 31st December 2021, page 53.

[3] Johnson & Johnson, Form 10-K, Fiscal year ended 1st January 2023, page 8.

[4] Abbott Laboratories, Form 10-K, Fiscal year ended 31st December 2022, page 6.

[5] GlaxoSmithKline, annual report, fiscal year ending 31st December 2021, page 275.

Bracing and chaos or general bloody-mindedness

By chance, I stumbled on the HM Revenue and Customs (HMRC) Annual Report and Accounts 2022 to 2023. I decided to read it to see if it would reveal anything interesting.

As a passing comment, I wonder why they choose to end their year on 31st March and not 5th April to follow the tax year that they make everyone else in the UK follow.

I have to admit, I read this document because of the recent reports of the extreme difficulty taxpayers are having in trying to contact a representative of HMRC. The level of service provided by HMRC to taxpayers has been atrocious for some time and remained so into 2024. It seems to me that either they cannot solve their problems or they don't care.

Here is but one of many articles that explain the situation, this one from *The Times*, entitled 'Brace yourself for more HMRC chaos', [1] which focuses on the postal backlog and delays in answering phone calls. HMRC management decided not to reply to letters less than a year old for several weeks in an attempt to reduce the backlog. This, of course, only creates more backlogs for later. In addition, would you believe, they refuse to answer emails.

I now compare this chaotic situation with their, oh so optimistic, Strategic Objective number 3 in their annual report: 'Maintain taxpayers' consent through fair treatment and protect society from harm.' They went on to explain how they performed. As you can imagine, there was no mention of bracing or chaos in their fair treatment. They were actually quite chuffed. They 'continue to make good progress' in how they have improved their 'customers' experience of interacting with' the HMRC. But surely, not replying to emails and letters cannot improve customer interaction. Rather, it eliminates it!

Still, on page 40, they do show us the results of a survey on 'Confidence in the way HMRC does its job'. Only 43% of individuals have confidence, meaning, of course, that 57% of individuals do not. This, I suggest, is not something to be proud of. And it is no better for the accountants and tax experts dealing with HMRC, as 65% of them do not have confidence. While HMRC attempt, but fail, to present these disastrous findings in the best possible light, at least they publish them. Credit to HRMC, despite their exaggeration that they 'continue to make good progress'.

HMRC do not consider their performance disastrous. They are happy. The overall score of 'customer satisfaction' is 79.2% of very satisfied or satisfied customers (page 47, if you don't believe me). No chaos here! Imagine how efficient they are elsewhere, with a result of only 54.1% of very satisfied or satisfied in their rather obscure service of 'Telephony'. I guess this result does not include those who didn't get through.

Finally, this example from *The Times* speaks volumes about HRMC's attitude, more than any percentage ever could:

> "One RSM accountant spent over six hours over the course of one week waiting on the general helpline with an urgent query to settle a client's outstanding tax liability. When HMRC eventually answered, it said it was unable to help and put the phone down. The client's payment deadline was missed." [1]

I can only think that this is general bloody-mindedness, even if the problem has arisen from lack of funding and lack of personnel. If they lack resources, they should be lenient to taxpayers not able to contact them. But they decide to be strict with taxpayers and lenient with themselves. As I said, bloody-mindedness.

But, even more interestingly, their attitude is not improving and, despite what they say, it seems they get pleasure in the difficulties they inflict on the taxpayer or they would have sorted out the problem. Another headline dated January 2024 speaks for itself:

"Accountants vent anger over HMRC's lack of care." [2]

[1] *The Times*, Brace yourself for more HMRC chaos, 20th May 2023, Rachel Mortimer, https://www.thetimes.co.uk/article/brace-yourself-for-more-hmrc-chaos-83nz3xcxw.

[2] *accountingWEB*, 22nd January 2024, Molly Macfarlane.

The not contingent non-liability

Contingent liabilities are not always contingent and are not always liabilities either.

This is another instance of accountants inventing an accounting term with no regard to the words used. It is true they use the term 'contingent liabilities' so often that its literal meaning has vanished, and people just recognise the term. Similar to a red bull. People no longer imagine a bull painted red standing alone in a field. They imagine a drink (some might imagine a Formula 1 racing car).

Contingent liabilities are not contingent on anything. They cannot be, because they either exist or are imaginary, or, to use the accounting expression, their 'existence will be confirmed' later. Later is contingent on something, but when the later existence becomes real, the amount becomes a real liability and no longer a contingent one. How about that for accounting magic?

Contingent liabilities are not liabilities either, because liabilities must be recorded in the balance sheet. As we all know, assets and liabilities make up a balance sheet, but not contingent liabilities. They are, as accountants say, an off-balance sheet item. They do not make up part of the results.

Here are the first eight words of the definition of a contingent liability: 'A contingent liability is a) a possible obligation ...' and it goes on '... or b) a present obligation ...'. So accountants know a contingent liability is an obligation, but they decide to call it a liability.

So we have two types of contingent liability: possible and present. Even here, accountants continue to mislead. Take, for example, the 'present' one, where essentially 'the amount ... cannot be measured with sufficient reliability', to use the words of the definition. Why use the word 'present' for something one cannot measure? Immeasurable might be better, but that is too explicit for accountants.

Contingent liabilities have another peculiarity. Although NOT part of the balance sheet, they have to be reported somewhere as part of the financial statements. Furthermore, the auditors must verify them. Most companies avoid this complication by tagging them on to the end of the financial statements in a note. Others sprinkle amounts throughout the financial statements as asides.

Some accountants agree with me that the term is misleading, and they never use it. Accountants in General Motors, for instance, do not use the term contingent liabilities in their 2022 annual report. They do, however, have 'Note 16 Commitments and Contingencies', where they resort to general disclaimers such as 'It is not possible to estimate our maximum exposure ...', or 'We are unable to estimate any reasonably possible material loss or range of loss that may result from ...'. They record contingent liabilities as required by the accounting standards but call them something else. They have even persuaded their auditors NOT to use the term contingent liability in their audit report.

For once, I am not alone. Many thanks to the accountants at General Motors for their passive resistance to the misleading term contingent liability.

How long does an aircraft fly?

One of the missions of IASB is to enhance international comparability of financial reports (I have put the full mission statement in Chapter 3 in the article 'A trusted global language worldwide'), but accountants cannot agree on how long an aircraft can fly. Or to use the standard accounting term the 'estimated useful life' of an aircraft. Accountants designed this term to be easy to understand and practical. It is both.

But they did not sufficiently define the term, so comparability vanishes. Estimated by whom? A technician at Airbus or Boeing, an accountant working in the airline company, or the barman serving drinks to an accountant's night out at the local pub? All of them qualify to make the estimation! Useful life.

Aircraft can fly for more than 30 years, sometimes even longer, so in theory they are useful for their maximum life. But no, accountants do not agree with this. I have taken information from three internationally known airlines, Singapore Airlines, British Airways and Air France, to compare the calculations of their estimated useful lives.

The maximum life of passenger aircraft is 20 years for Singapore Airlines. These same aircraft last nine years longer when flown by British Airways pilots, at 29 years, while Air France fall between the two, at 25 years.

Sometimes, though, aircraft stop working before their maximum lifespan. Those flying with Singapore Airlines only seem to last 12 years, whereas British Airways aircraft never have to be scrapped before their 25th birthday. Quite amazing! Their useful life is more than double their Singaporean cousins. And then, even more incredible, the maximum useful life of Singapore Airlines passenger aircraft is the same as Air France's minimum.

What about the average useful lives? We of course have no information but, by averaging the maximums and minimums, we find an average useful life for Singapore Airlines of 16 years, for British Airways of 27 years, and for Air France of 22.5 years.

Things are no better for the residual value at the end of their useful lives. We have no information for Air France. Perhaps zero? It is up to 10% for Singapore Airlines, depending on something we are not told about, and up to 5% for British Airways, again without telling us what the criteria are for fixing the rates. But then, who really cares?

I would have thought the easiest way to calculate the estimated useful life and residual value of aircraft would be to consult the company that manufactured them. None of the accountants in these three companies seem to have done that, or they talked to different experts in the same company who gave different estimates. They certainly didn't talk to other accountants in the industry. They did what was useful for their company regardless of others, resulting in a significant difference in depreciation charges. So comparability does not work.

Chapter 6

The Most Boring Book in the World

The most boring book in the world is a bestseller but you won't find it on any bestseller list. Its subject matter is perfect for boredom. It costs an expensive €120, so it's profitable for the publisher. It has 607 pages and has been translated into many languages. Its style is perfectly adapted to make you fall asleep after a couple of paragraphs. But even here it fails. The book is so heavy that, as soon as sleep comes on, it falls out of your hands and wakes you up with a start. The title of this book is *OECD Transfer Pricing Guidelines for Multinational Enterprises and Tax Administrations*, January 2022. [1] You really don't want to read it, even if you know what 'transfer pricing' is. I surprised even myself by finding things to write about.

I start with the title of Chapter 1: 'The Arm's Length Principle'.

This has nothing to do with measuring the distance between a wrist and a shoulder. The term 'length of an arm' was shortened back in the 14th century to 'arm's length', when it seems to have obtained an additional meaning, that of independence or lack of intimacy. So it has been around for more than 450 years.

The OECD then made it into a principle. They could have called it 'The Principle of the Length of an Arm' or 'The Principle of the Weight of a Leg.' But no, they chose the shortened version, which, it is true, does sound better: 'The Arm's Length Principle'. It takes them over 60 pages to explain it.

The price of a transfer

This book is remarkable in its clarity and detail on the principles and practices of transfer pricing. It is also remarkable in its failure to prevent large multinational companies from paying their fair share of taxes worldwide. Or, to put it more simply, its purpose is to identify tax loopholes. Unfortunately, it does no such thing.

Transfer pricing policies may be used for 'tax fraud and tax avoidance'. This is a timid attempt to appear fair to both enterprises and tax authorities. But it is not just timid, it is also untrue. Transfer pricing policies are always used for tax avoidance, and sometimes even for tax fraud. Everyone knows that.

During my CFO career, I was forced to read sections of the book to counter the threats of an enthusiastic tax inspector, who proclaimed he was going to recover millions of undeclared taxes and force the company to pay substantial fines. He implied that we were not applying the rules in the OECD guidelines. My ardent tax man had missed the one sentence in the book written especially for him:

> "Tax administrations should not automatically assume that associated enterprises have sought to manipulate profits and avoid taxation." (Chapter 1, Paragraph A1.2, Page 29)

I suspect none of the tax administrations worldwide have read this sentence either. Or, if they have, they choose to ignore it. Tax administrations always consider that enterprises are out to **manipulate** profits to minimise taxes. Enterprises consider they are out to **adjust** profits to minimise taxes, not to manipulate them. Why pay more tax than you need to?

From this conflictual position comes the wide divergence in opinion between tax authorities and taxpayers. The authors are honest enough to state that the whole system of transfer pricing has 'too much room for interpretation'. So they admit their rules are not precise enough!

Comparing the potential

Read the following sentence without trying to understand it, because it is incomprehensible to us ordinary mortals.

> "In practice, both quantitative and qualitative criteria are used to include or reject potential comparables." [1]

Imagine reaching page 161, with sentence after sentence like this one. Common everyday words are used. But they are deployed in ways that even someone who understands the issues will find largely impenetrable.

One can, perhaps, guess what a comparable is, but who knows what it means in this context, let alone a potential comparative? And then why would anyone want to use criteria to include or reject comparables? To include in what? To reject from what? And to make it more bewildering the authors explain nothing.

But what is amazing, in this simple sentence of 15 words, is that they manage to enumerate six alternatives. That is quite an achievement. Here they are:

1) Quantitative criteria to include
2) Quantitative criteria to reject
3) Qualitative criteria to include
4) Qualitative criteria to reject
5) Both quantitative and qualitative criteria to include
6) Both quantitative and qualitative criteria to reject

They have managed to make a relatively simple sentence difficult to understand. Imagine what they achieve with the complex ones! I have included one below as an example from page 267 on the subject of funding intangibles:

> "The higher the development risk and the closer the financial risk is related to the development risk, the more the funder will need to have the capacity to assess the progress of the development of the intangible and the consequences of this progress for achieving its expected funding return, and the closer the funder may link the continued provision of funding to key operational developments that may impact its financial risk."

Imagine finding this on page 267 and glancing down to realise you've still got 340 pages to go! Luckily, I did find some lighter moments, albeit few and far between, in this reading marathon.

Arms and thumbs

On page 95, the authors bring up arms and thumbs. Take this short sentence:

> "Accordingly, a rule of thumb cannot be used to evidence that a price or an arrangement of income is arm's length."

It's a pity they are inconsistent. They should either use 'thumb's rule' with 'arm's length' or 'rule of thumb' with 'length of an arm', and not mix up the expressions. It makes it untidy and rather unwieldy! And what on earth is an 'arrangement of income'? I have no idea and, even if I did, I would not bore you with an explanation.

Berries

In an attempt to relieve the boredom, the authors introduce fruit into their text. But one has to wait until page 125 to find it, by which time its main use is as a palate cleanser, no doubt. They should have included it in Chapter 1.

Now, I am not being fair in suggesting fruit as the subject, but it came to mind while reading, in the unconscious attempt of my brain to stay concentrated. It comes from the name of an obscure financial ratio, the berry ratio, which the authors introduce into their transfer pricing to show their accounting expertise.

Berry ratios are named after an American economist, Charles Berry, who invented them in 1979. As such, they have nothing at all to do with fruit; you cannot precede them with 'straw', 'ras' or 'black', unfortunately. The ratio compares a company's gross profit to its operating expenses. I have never used it, nor had I ever heard of it until I reached this page. Some accountants think it is a 'shady' ratio. [2] I agree.

Poetry again

The authors do throw in alliteration from time to time, in an attempt, no doubt, to compete with accounting standards. But they fail; I find them quite inadequate.

They introduce the first one early, on the third page of the first chapter, page 31:

> "… conditions which would have obtained between independent enterprises in comparable transactions and comparable circumstances (i.e. in 'comparable uncontrollable transactions') …"

Too many 'comparables' make for a poor man's alliteration. It's really just repetition.

I include another with an obsession with the letter 'p':

> "Specifically, it is important to consider the actual and potential profitability of products or potential products that are based on the intangible."

Five 'p's in this one on page 297, where they lose the poetic effect with the repetition of 'products' and 'potential'. I cannot imagine what they mean by a potential product.

Here is another with 'p':

> "In some cases, taxpayers will regularly prepare financial projections for business planning purposes."

This one has a better poetic ring to it. And they go wild in the same paragraph with nine 'p's in this sentence:

> "It is usually the case that projections prepared for non-tax business planning purposes are more reliable than projections prepared exclusively for tax purposes or exclusively for purposes of a transfer pricing analysis."

The authors have difficulty with assonance. They wait until page 109 to give us this short, sharp sentence:

> "Another important aspect of comparability is accounting consistency."

Safe in the harbour

I have to admit, I did not know what a transfer price 'safe harbour' was until I reached page 203. It has nothing to do with tying up boats to keep them safe.

But not content to adopt the usual tax meaning, the authors invent something complicated. They repeat the tactic they use in the arm's length principle. They then massacre the original meaning of 'safe harbour' on page 493 by creating a 'bilateral safe harbour MOU'.

No, I don't know what a bilateral safe harbour MOU is and I have no wish to learn, as I am sure you don't either. Let's leave it there, but to add the words 'bilateral' and 'MOU' to safe harbour is too much. An MOU, by the way, means a memorandum of understanding.

Methods of transfer pricing

I will leave you with the strange names the authors have dreamed up for the five different methods of transfer pricing:

> CUP: Comparable uncontrolled price method
> Resale price method
> Cost plus method
> TNMM: Transactional net margin method
> Transactional profit split method

But, having explained each method in incredible detail, the authors then systematically make their mea culpa and explain how difficult each one is to apply.

In the CUP, for instance, they state:

> "It may be **difficult** to find a transaction between independent enterprises that is similar enough to a controlled transaction …"

For the resale price method:

> "There could well be practical **difficulties** in obtaining this information …"
> "The cost plus method presents some **difficulties** in proper application, particularly in determining the costs."

So they invent a method with costs that are too difficult to determine. How about that?

In the TNMM:

> "These aspects make accurate and reliable determination of arm's length net profit indicators difficult."

And finally:

> "A weakness of the transactional profit split method relates to difficulties in application."

The authors then give three examples where it would seem, most of the time, that information is not available or is so difficult to obtain it cannot be applied in practice.

Every single method is difficult in some way or another. I guess one has to congratulate the authors on their honesty, but to write a book that explains methods that are so deficient and yet followed throughout the world says something about accountants and tax experts. It all comes down to judgement – the judgement of the company accountants against the judgement of a country's tax authorities. That explains transfer pricing and why accountants and tax inspectors never agree.

My favourite method has to be the cup – not saucer, not mug, but CUP in capitals. They introduce this acronym, to lighten the atmosphere a little because, by Chapter 2, the book is difficult to read. They also throw in a similar one to the CUP, the MAP, which isn't a map either. A MAP is a Mutual Agreement Procedure.

[1] The official reference to the book is the following, or to quote: 'Please cite this reference as: OECD (2022), OECD *Transfer Pricing Guidelines for Multinational Enterprises and Tax Administrations*, 2022, OECD Publishing, Paris, https://doi.org/10.1787/0e655865-en'.

[2] You will find this reference on the site Investopedia under the title 'Berry Ratio', written by Will Kenton.

Chapter 7

Reaching Ridiculous

Revelation of company-specific risks

I thought I was being clever when I analysed the risk statements of the eight pharmaceutical companies to find and isolate company-specific risks. I claimed that companies hide these risks in the mass of rubbish called risk statements. I was wrong. I only found four, two of them in Sanofi, and one common to two companies. This means the eight pharmaceutical companies share common risks or, more likely, they copy each other's, ensuring risk statements continue to be bland and worthless.

Sanofi's two company-specific risks:

Contamination

Sanofi state they have risks of 'historical contamination related to our past industrial activities' in which they 'may become involved in claims, lawsuits and administrative proceedings …'. But they stop there and give no more information.

I found no evidence of possible claims, lawsuits or administrative proceedings elsewhere in their annual report, so all they do by including this risk as a material one is make me worry about the real value of the shares I hold.

Shareholder

Then they give us the information that their largest shareholder, L'Oréal, owns 16.78% of the voting rights of Sanofi and that affiliates of L'Oréal serve on the board of directors. As a result, L'Oréal remains in a position to exert greater influence in the appointment of the directors and in other actions that require shareholders' approval.

This statement could have been placed elsewhere in the annual report as information in the way that, for instance, AbbVie do. But Sanofi decide to classify it as a material risk, which I find rather odd. It raises more questions than answers. Are they losing confidence in L'Oréal, or is L'Oréal exerting too much pressure on Sanofi? Nobody knows. And we will never know unless an eventual clash becomes public.

Risks common to two companies

But I did find a risk common to two companies in what they call separation.

If Johnson & Johnson mess up their separation of a large part of their business, they consider this a risk:

> "The planned separation of the Company's Consumer Health business may not be completed on the terms or timeline currently contemplated, if at all, and may not achieve the expected results."

The risks they state are impressive: the costs to complete will be significant, the financial benefits may not be met, the anticipated benefits may prove incorrect, the share price may fluctuate, the common stock may become volatile, the Internal Revenue Service may not agree with the proposed tax-free nature of the transaction, and so it goes on. One wonders why they even want to separate out their Consumer Health business with this level of uncertainty.

GSK are also into separation, by creating a consumer health business, but they are not as worried as Johnson & Johnson. They explain that they have set up an FRO – to plan, monitor and carry out the separation – and that this FRO reports in every month to GLT. All is well, no need to worry, FRO and GLT will resolve any problems so this cannot be a risk.

You might be asking what FRO and GLT stand for. FRO is Future Ready Office and GLT stands for GSK Leadership Team, and I remind you, GSK stands for GlaxoSmithKline. FRO, as you can imagine, made me smile. What a frivolous name for such a serious management team. And to call it 'Office' gives me the impression, at the mundane level, they are moving into a new building, and the use of 'future ready' makes them sound like time travellers – building prototypes of spaceships.

Jargon construction

You will have realised by now how rather indignant I am at the two accounting boards, FASB and IASB. I don't know why I bother with this emotion, but I am settled now. (I use the term my son uses on his dog, Spritz, when he gets excited – Settle! Settle!) Writing about their odd behaviour towards each other must have settled me.

Accountants write abundantly among themselves about the differences between the accounting standards prepared by the FASB and the IASB. These articles warn shareholders that results may be different depending on the accounting standards that apply. But we will never know by how much, because the only way to find out is to prepare two sets of accounts: one under FASB standards and the other under IASB ones.

Would you believe some companies do this? They have to, but only at the subsidiary level. For instance, a subsidiary in Europe of a US parent company prepares local financial statements under IASB standards, but sends different financial statements to the parent company under FASB standards. Auditors audit both sets and announce they are both fairly stated, but not to the same person; the parent company receives results under the FASB standards, and the local directors under IASB.

Now that I am settled, I am able to analyse the effect of differences between the FASB and the IASB. This reveals the two boards have developed four secret habits, common to accountants in their use of jargon:

1) They give different meanings to the same word (probable, material).
2) They agree on an accounting term but make different interpretations of its meaning (Chief Operating Decision Maker, subsequent event).

3) They use different expressions to mean the same thing (true and fair/presents fairly, substantial doubt/significant doubt).
4) They give ordinary English words different meanings to the ones we generally use (inputs, joints).

The accounting profession often use this last habit in their jargon. As I have shown, they give meanings to 'headroom' and 'clean' that differ from the ones we generally use. This is like deciding to call an accounting term 'cat' and explaining in the definition that it barks.

Let's take another example, 'cut-off'. Cut-off, as an accounting term, doesn't cut or separate anything. Nor is it dangerous or sharp. Nor has it any relation to the well-known figurative expression 'cut off your nose to spite your face'. Accountants decree cut-off to be the accounting term that shows whether income and expenses are recorded in the correct period. They figuratively cut the old year on the last day at midnight, before starting off the new year in the next second. The term, cut-off, seems logical to them.

My favourite

I end with my ultimate favourite. I thought I had already written too much on going concern, when by chance, I found a report written by the IAASB. I laughed out loud the first time I read it. The writers believe in what they have written, and the board members still don't see the funny side, or they would have taken it down from their site.

The IAASB set up the Going Concern Task Force to publish answers to the most frequently asked questions on going concern. Now, would you believe me if I told you this is the first, most frequently asked question on going concern?

> *"What is the purpose of MURGC and KAM sections and EOM paragraphs in the auditor's report?"*

This is not a joke. We are in the real world of audit and assurance.

The report in question is entitled Frequently Asked Questions, August 2022, Reporting Going Concern Matters in the Auditor's Report. It shows how sincere and serious accountants end up making fools of themselves. A classic.

Please note that KAM has nothing to do with a Key Account Manager in this context. It is a Key Auditing Matter. And EOM is not End of Month, nor is it End of Message. It is not the Employee of the Month either and has nothing to do with the well-known medical expression Extra-Ocular Movement, nor any of the other 25 recognised meanings. Auditors have invented yet another EOM to keep people guessing: Emphasis of Matter. Of course!

So what is going on here? Auditors have taken two popular acronyms, KAM and EOM, given them new meanings and associated them with MURGC. What percentage of qualified accountants worldwide knows what MURGC means? Close to zero, I am certain. Until I had read this report of the IAASB, I had no idea what it meant either. MURGC is, of course, 'Material Uncertainty Relating to Going Concern'.

You should also note I didn't read the answer to this amazing question. Even if, I am sure, it could give me mounds of additional subjects to write about, my curiosity does not extend this far. And I am afraid I wouldn't understand it.

But the task force members don't stop at Question 1; they dig their embarrassing hole deeper and insist in Question 4:

"What is the interrelationship between MURGC, KAM and EOM?"

It sounds like a trick question in an accounting exam:

"You have three hours to answer the question in no more than 3,000 words. Please write on one side of the paper only, put your name in the top right-hand corner of each page and remember to number the pages. Do not forget to explain what MURGC, KAM and EOM mean before answering the question. You may not consult ISA 700, ISA 701, ISA 706 or ISA 570 during the exam."

With these two questions, I ask myself, have the IAASB chosen the right title for their publication: 'Frequently Asked Questions, August 2022'?

'Frequently' is the wrong word here. 'Infrequently' does not do justice to the questions either. 'Rarely' would be better. But then who would ever read a publication with the title 'Rarely Asked Questions, August 2022'? They should have chosen the title 'Questions never asked about going concern'!

I'm satisfied at last. My search for the silliest in the serious ends in style with the ridiculous.

Annex 1

Surprise Certificate

Here's what I posted back in April 2021 when I received the letter from the ICAEW:

> I received a surprise certificate today from the Institute of Chartered Accountants in England and Wales: recognition on reaching 50 years of membership. I don't know how I should feel.
>
> Should I feel proud? Proud for perseverance? Or grateful for getting there? Satisfaction, but for what exactly? Delighted? Honoured for my age? I certainly feel old! Should I open a bottle of champagne for breakfast and just accept the congratulations? It's true, managing to stay a chartered accountant for 50 years, yet still posting on LinkedIn, is an achievement in itself. Should I simply thank the President directly – he signed it after all?
>
> And then, what should I do with the certificate? Frame it and hang it on the wall in the hall beside my ACA qualification certificate from 1971? It has survived my numerous moves intact, but in its third frame. Or should I put it in a drawer to be found when I next move house? Not sure.
>
> Finally, all I will do is tell the LinkedIn world and my blog and see what happens! Hopefully nothing – but it was fun writing about it. Many thanks to the Institute.

I received genuine enthusiasm from my fellow accountants on LinkedIn, but the reactions of a few non-accountants were different. There were some who wondered whether it was not a 'Commiserations Certificate'. They seem to think I should be in a state of personal sorrow, working as an accountant for 50 years. How can anyone last that long in such a profession?

Commiseration is, I think, too strong. Sympathy is kinder. A 'Sympathy Certificate' instead. Sympathy for the stamina required to work as a chartered accountant for 50 years? I can accept sympathy but not commiseration.

The original is still in the drawer of my desk and the certificate has finally found a home on the back cover of my book.

Acknowledgements

Writing is a solitary activity, but towards the end a whole team of people agreed to help me get the book onto the shelves. Many thanks to Julia Sandford-Cooke and John Ingamells, who advised me when to clarify my message, and when to adjust my attempts at humour; to Rhiannon James who read the whole book to keep me out of trouble; to Helen Hart and her team at SilverWood Books in Bristol; and to Florence Bret for her marvellous drawings.

Milton Keynes UK
Ingram Content Group UK Ltd.
UKHW031310261024
450183UK00003B/60